Making
Stylish
Belts

Making Stylish Belts

Do-it-Yourself Projects to Craft and Sew at Home

Ellen Goldstein-Lynch, Nicole Malone, and Sarah Mullins
OF THE ACCESSORIES DESIGN DEPARTMENT AT THE FASHION INSTITUTE OF TECHNOLOGY

QUARRY BOOKS

BEVERLY MASSACHUSETTS

© 2007 by Quarry Books

All rights reserved. No part of this book may be reproduced in any
form without written permission of the copyright owners. All images
in this book have been reproduced with the knowledge and prior
consent of the artists concerned, and no responsibility is accepted by
the producer, publisher, or printer for any infringement of copyright
or otherwise, arising from the contents of this publication. Every
effort has been made to ensure that credits accurately comply with
information supplied. We apologize for any inaccuracies that may
have occurred and will resolve inaccurate or missing information in
a subsequent reprinting of the book.

First published in the United States of America by
Quarry Books, a member of
Quayside Publishing Group
100 Cummings Center
Suite 406-L
Beverly, Massachusetts 01915-6101
Telephone: (978) 282-9590
Fax: (978) 283-2742
www.quarrybooks.com

Library of Congress Cataloging-in-Publication Data
Goldstein-Lynch, Ellen.
  Making stylish belts : do-it-yourself projects to craft and sew at home / Ellen
Goldstein-Lynch, Nicole Malone, and Sarah Mullins.
    p. cm.
  ISBN 1-59253-372-8 (pbk.)
  1. Belts (Clothing) 2. Fancy work. I. Malone, Nicole. II. Mullins, Sarah. III. Title.

  TT668.G54 2007
  646.4'8--dc22

                                                                    2007010925

ISBN-13: 978-1-59253-372-5
ISBN-10: 1-59253-372-8

10 9 8 7 6 5 4 3 2 1

Design: Laura H. Couallier, Laura Herrmann Design
Cover Image: Glenn Scott, Glenn Scott Photography
Illustrations: Judy Love
Patterns: Roberta Frauwirth
Technical Editor: Christine Timmons

Printed in China

❧ CONTENTS ❧

❧ INTRODUCTION ☙

If you open any woman's closet on any given day, you're bound to discover at least two or three, and possibly many more, belts. Today, a belt is considered one of the must-haves for any fashionista's wardrobe. Formerly, the belt was designated as a functional accessory and consisted of nothing more than a strip of leather and a buckle, with the leather available only in black, brown, or tan, and the buckle made of brass or silver.

Belts are now one of fashion's most sought-after accessories. They can completely change the look of an outfit by adding dimension or accentuating the positive. They come in every color, shape, and style imaginable. Having a lot of belts in different colors is almost like having a fashion box of crayons. You just never know which one will suit your mood, change your look, or create the right illusion.

Have you ever gone into a store and looked at a belt on a mannequin that was to die for and thought to yourself, "Maybe I can make that." Well, you can!

In these pages, you'll find the inspiration and information you need to create amazing belts—some involving little or no sewing (including ideas for turning ho-hum store-bought belts into works of art), and others requiring just a little sewing skill.

The instructions for all the belts are easy to follow, the patterns concise and easy to read, and the projects exciting. We've also included a gallery of belts to show you just what you can achieve by building on the various basic projects in this book and to offer further inspiration and design ideas.

Making Stylish Belts offers inspired handmade solutions that will complement or add pizzazz to any outfit. You'll find great no-sew projects that would be fast and fun to make with a group of crafty friends and that are perfect even for the younger set— Girl Scout or Brownie troops, high-school classes, or campers. All of the projects would make great birthday, holiday, and any-day gifts and can be customized to suit any style.

Making Stylish Belts will tickle your fancy and excite your creative mind. So what are you waiting for? Clear off the dining room table; pull out your favorite fabrics, trims, and embellishments; sharpen your scissors; get out the glue; turn up the volume on your favorite CD; and get going! A wardrobe full of wonderful belts awaits you.

—Ellen Goldstein-Lynch, Nicole Malone, and Sarah Mullins, Fashion Institute of Technology, New York City

CHAPTER 1
❧ GETTING STARTED ❧

ESSENTIAL TOOLS

ESSENTIAL TOOLS

You don't need a fully equipped sewing room or design studio to make amazing belts. All you need are a few basic tools and supplies—and some imagination. In this book, we've focused on two different types of belts: those that require little or no sewing at all, and those that require just a little simple sewing. To construct both types of belts, you'll need to find a **clean, flat surface** to work on. A folding table, kitchen table, or sewing table is perfect. Just make sure that the table is solid and doesn't wobble. Also, be sure when you're working that the surface is free of food and dirt. You wouldn't want your latest creation to be destroyed by coffee, tea, or a candy bar, would you? By the way, if you're like us and tend to work on the dining room table, make sure to protect it with a pad or a lightweight cutting board.

A Needle-Nose Pliers B Mallet C Hammer D Rotary Cutter E Metal Ruler F Rotary Hole Punch G 69 Nylon Thread H Rivet- and Snap-Setting Kit I Top: Gauge Foot, Middle: Teflon Foot, Bottom: Zipper Foot J Hole Punch K Oval Punch L Rivet Setter M Binder Clips N Grommet Setter O Awl P Bone Folder Q Craft Knife R Seam Ripper S Magnetic Snap and Washers T Turn Lock U Buckle V D-Ring, O-Ring W Grommet and Washer X Rivet Y Collar Pin Set Z Lacing Needle and Glover's Needle

The next issue is lighting. Without the **proper lighting**, your eyes will play tricks on you. Natural light is always best, but if you don't have the luxury of working in a window-filled room, don't worry. Just make sure that you have sufficient light. But how do you know if the light is sufficient? It's simple: Don't work in your own shadow. And, if you can't see everything on the table, add more light!

For the projects that require sewing, you'll definitely need a **sewing machine** of some kind. The particular style doesn't really matter, as long as you're comfortable using it. A new computerized sewing machine or a thirty-year-old workhorse will do the trick. Just make sure that the machine you choose is in good working order.

When working with craft or fabric glues, even hot glue, you'll want to work near a window or have the air conditioning on so that you have **proper ventilation**. Make sure to use fresh glue. If the glue has been in your closet for six months or more, toss it.

Next, if you're working with fabric and it's wrinkled, you'll need a good **steam iron**. As with the sewing machine, the brand or style of iron doesn't matter, provided it does the job.

No craftsperson can ever have too many pairs of **scissors**. You may want one pair for cutting fabric and another for cutting leather. Just make sure that your scissors are always sharp and that they're comfortable in your hand. You can also use a **rotary cutter** for cutting fabric and leather, so you might want to get one of those (and extra blades) too. And don't forget a sharp pair of **pinking shears** for decorative detailing and sharp **utility and craft knives** for cutting leather. It's also a good idea to have a **steel or metal ruler** to use as a guide when cutting leather belts to prevent injury. This type of ruler comes in a 48" (122 cm) length, which is perfect for making leather belts.

Another essential is the right type of **thread**. For belts, use a nylon, polyester, or polyester/cotton blend—whichever works best in your machine.

Sewing machine **needles** are another must-have. Make sure that you have a range of sizes for stitching different fabrics or for sewing with decorative threads. And while on the subject of needles, don't forget hand-sewing needles. For embroidery, use an embroidery needle; for beading on leather, use a glover's needle; for beading on fabric, use a beading needle; for lacing on leather, use a lacing needle. And remember to change all your needles regularly.

You'll also need **straight pins** for pinning fabric and decorative trims in place.

Pins come in various types and sizes. Choose whatever type and size you find most comfortable to work with, but make sure that the pins are long enough to go through the fabric.

Double-sided craft tape is great for turning under edges of fabric or temporarily adhering pieces of fabric before sewing. It's often better than glue because it eliminates the risk of having glue seep onto the fabric and stain it. Another handy type of tape is regular **masking tape or painter's tape** (that blue tape). Both can be very helpful when working on leather and suede belts.

Don't forget to have an ample supply of **fabric-marking pens and pencils**, including **water- and air-soluble markers,** for tracing patterns and marking fabrics.

A **snap- and grommet-setting kit, a hole punch**, and **needle-nose pliers** are also key tools when working with leather and suede projects. We recommend that you add them to your tool kit if you haven't already.

BELT VOCABULARY

- The **belt tip** is the front section of the belt that goes through the belt buckle.

- The **belt point** refers to the shape of the belt tip, and there are seven basic belt points: Bullet, Round, Straight-end, V-point, Rounded-corner, Half-round and Hanky-point.

- A **keeper** is a loop of leather, fabric, plastic, or metal that holds the belt tip flat against the belt after the tip feeds through the buckle.

- A **harness buckle** is a buckle whose bar is located on the left or right side of the buckle.

- A **center-bar buckle** is a buckle whose bar is located in the center of the buckle.

- A **prong** is a metal spike on a buckle that is inserted into the belt's size hole.

- A **size hole** is the center hole of usually three to five holes punched in the belt-tip end.

- A **prong slot** is an oval or rectangular slot punched or cut into the belt wrap to accommodate the belt buckle's prong.

- A **belt wraparound** is an additional $1^1/2$" to 3" (4–7.5 cm) on the end of the belt that wraps around the buckle bar and is riveted or stitched to hold the buckle.

BUCKLES

Belts are all about color, materials, embellishments, and style. But they're also about buckles—and choosing the right buckle is key.

There are two basic types of buckles: a **harness buckle** and a **center-bar buckle**. The harness buckle always needs a belt loop, or keeper, to hold the belt closed. The center-bar buckle usually (though not always) has a part that keeps the belt closed and hence doesn't need a belt loop, or keeper.

When making a belt with a prong, always make an odd number of holes, because a belt should be worn on the center size hole. With regard to the number of holes on a belt, the rule of thumb is that three holes are used on expensive belts; five holes on moderately priced belts; and seven holes on men's belts, Western-style belts, and unisex belts.

BELT VOCABULARY

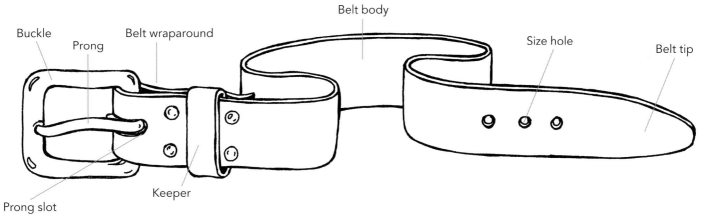

Buckle · Prong · Belt wraparound · Belt body · Size hole · Belt tip

Prong slot · Keeper

HARNESS BUCKLE

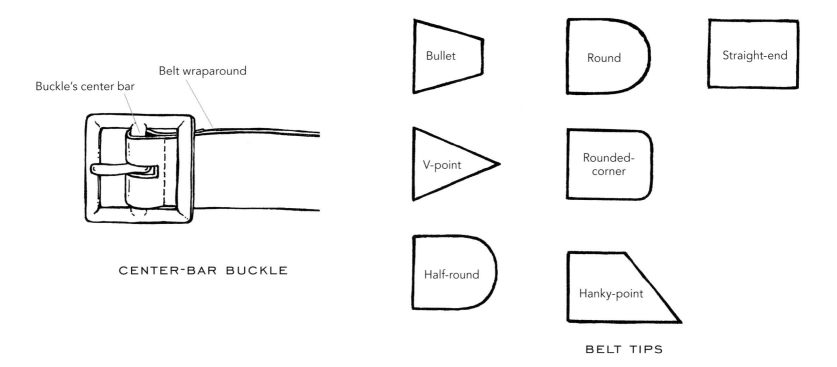

Buckle's center bar · Belt wraparound

CENTER-BAR BUCKLE

Bullet · Round · Straight-end

V-point · Rounded-corner

Half-round · Hanky-point

BELT TIPS

BASIC BELT TECHNIQUES

A number of the projects in this book require some simple skills: punching holes, setting rivets and grommets, and adding collar pins. The following illustrations take you through each of these techniques.

PUNCHING A BASIC HOLE

1. Place punch over leather and hit with mallet.

USING AN OVAL LEATHER PUNCH ▶

1. Place oval punch in desired location and hit with mallet.

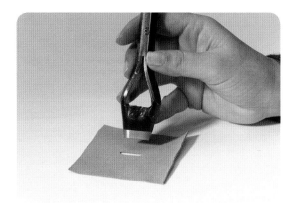

2. Remove punch.

SETTING A RIVET   ▶   ▶

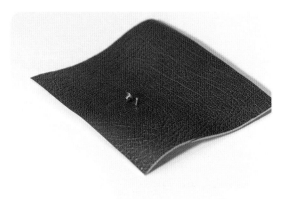

1. Assemble materials and punch hole.

2. Place rivet post through hole, push rivet cap onto post, and hammer rivet setter over cap to set.

3. Remove setter and check that rivet is securely set.

SETTING A GROMMET

1. After hole is punched, place grommet through hole from front. Position grommet on anvil, right-side down. Place washer over grommet on wrong side.

2. Place setter into grommet and hit with mallet.

3. Remove setter and check that grommet is securely set.

ADDING A COLLAR PIN

1. After punching hole, place screw through hole from bottom.

2. Screw collar pin on.

FASHION, FIT, AND STYLING

If the belt fits, wear it! But if the belt sparkles and has a mind of its own, flaunt it!

The right belt can really bring an outfit together. And any humble ensemble—whether a T-shirt and jeans, a white blouse and skirt, or a simple black dress—can be elevated to a whole new level of style with the right fantastic belt.

But before you get started making any of the many included in this book, let us give you some fashion-savvy information about belts that will help you decide on just the right ones to make for your favorite outfits.

Belts are sold in stores and boutiques and also by street vendors in many cities, and most belts are sized to fit waist measurements. Women's belts run from 22" to 34" (56–86.5 cm) in length (unless the belt

is meant to wrap twice around the waist). Some belts are sized as small, medium, large, and extra-large, while others are adjustable and are one-size-fits-all.

Men's belts are also sized by waist measurements: small (30" to 32" [76–81.5 cm]), medium (34" to 36" [86.5–91.5 cm]), medium-large (38" to 40" [96.5–101.5 cm]), and large (42" to 44" [106.5–112 cm]).

Belts are made from a variety of materials, including leather, suede, reptile and other exotic skins, wooden or plastic links, plastic strips, straws, and all types of fabrics—some even made of fabric to coordinate with a garment. Jeweled, beaded, or sequined belts have often been designated as evening accessories, but today the trend is for more dazzle for both day and evening. Wide ribbon and fabrics can be used for sashes. And buckles can be made of wood, metal, or plastic and also covered to coordinate with a garment.

Now that you know about the sizing of belts and the materials used to make them, let's look at the different types of belts:

- An **adjustable belt** refers to a one-size belt that fits all bodies. It can be resized by removing the buckle and cutting the belt down or by using side ratchets if the buckle has them.

- A **bandolier belt** is worn over the shoulder and torso rather than around the waist.

- A **belt bag** is a belt with an attached or detachable pouch.

- A **Boy Scout belt** is made of canvas, twill, or webbed material and has a self-adjusting slide buckle. It comes in one size and is usually cut to fit.

- **Suspenders**, or **braces**, are a Y-shaped support that goes over the shoulders and attaches to trousers at the center-back waist and to the left and right front waist to hold the trousers up (or just to add a decorative fashion accent to both trousers and skirts). Traditionally, suspenders button to the inside of a trouser waistband, but some may fasten with clips instead. Suspenders can be made of elastic, webbing, or other materials, and they can be solid or patterned and fashioned for men, women, and children.

- A **cartridge belt** has a series of either cylindrical loops or pockets. These loops or pockets were originally sewn on the belt to hold ammunition.

- A **cinch belt**, or **waist cincher**, is a wide, tight belt that accents the waist and is often made of stretch elastic.

- A **contour belt** is a wide belt cut to conform to the shape of the figure.

- A **corset** is a wide belt similar to a waist cincher. The corset often curves above and below the waist and can buckle or lace up the front. The lace-up version is also known as a Merry Widow corselet.

- A **cowboy belt** is stiff and made of tooled leather and usually has a metal buckle. The cowboy belt became very popular in recent decades, thanks to the revival of Western wear.

- A **cummerbund** is a wide, sashlike belt made of pleated fabric. It's usually worn by men with formal or evening attire.

- A **dangle belt** is any belt with decorations hanging from it.

- A **dog-leash belt** resembles a dog's leash with the same type of spring-loaded snap closure a leash has.

- A **fish-scale belt** is made of stretch metallic material that looks as if it's made of fish scales. This type of belt was quite popular in the 1970s.

- A **lariat** is a woven belt, usually made of leather, that looks like a cowboy's rope. Again, this type of belt has become very popular, thanks to the Western revival.

- A **link belt** is any belt made of interlocking links, such as a chain belt.

- A **metallic belt** is any metal belt, including a link belt.

- An **obi** is a wide sash adapted from the traditional Japanese sash worn over a kimono. It is usually 12' to 15' (3.7–4.6 m) long and wraps around the waist, knotted and arranged in a bowlike fold on the back.

- A **polo belt** is a stiff belt with front straps, which is adapted from the types of belts worn by polo players.

- A **rope belt** is a cord belt that can be wrapped around the waist and tied.

- A **sash belt** is made of soft fabric or ribbon and wrapped around the waist and tied.

- A **self-belt** is made of the same fabric as the garment it's intended to be worn with. It can be styled as a sash, adjustable, cinch, or wrap belt.

- A **tack belt** is a leather belt with a narrower piece sewn on the front to fit through the buckle.

- And, lastly, a **wrap belt** is one that wraps around the waist and is either tied or buckled. It can be made in various materials and widths.

BASIC BELT CONSTRUCTION

There are two basic types of belt constructions: a **raw-edge belt** and a **turned-edge belt**. The raw-edge belt looks like a sandwich, with each component laid on top of the previous layer and all the layers visible along the edge. By contrast, a turned-edge belt has a smooth-finished edge with only the outermost layer visible. You'll find the basic construction methods for each belt on the following pages. Start to perfect your skills by completing one of each type of belt, so that you'll already have an established pattern and finished sample to refer to when you find one of these techniques referred to in a project.

Raw-edge belt

Turned-edge belt

RAW-EDGE
❧ BELT ❧

MATERIALS

Note: Firm, non-stretchy leathers, such as cowhide, would be most suitable for this project.

one strip of light- to medium-weight leather for outside of belt (strip's width and length should be at least ½" [1.3 cm] larger all around than pattern you make)

one strip of light- to medium-weight leather for lining of belt (cut same size as outside strip)

one strip of belt filler material, ideally bonded leather; firm, thin strip of scrap leather can be substituted (cut same size as previous strips). *Note: Filler can be omitted if outside and lining leathers are of substantial weight.*

rubber cement

masking tape (or pattern weights)

one center-bar or harness buckle

one to four rivets (one or two for center-bar buckle, depending on belt's width; two to four for harness buckle); length of rivet posts should just fit through thickness of belt doubled over on itself

thread for machine sewing

TOOLS

long piece of pattern paper (thick, manila-type paper works best)

utility or craft knife

awl

scissors

rotary or handheld hole punch, size #1 (³⁄₃₂" [2.5 mm]) for rivets

oblong punch (size should fit buckle prong)

48" (122 cm) metal ruler

12" (30.5 cm) metal ruler

rivet-setting kit

plier stapler

rawhide mallet or hammer

long cutting mat

cardboard or thick leather to place under belt when using handheld punches

edge dye or acrylic paint with paintbrush or dauber (optional)

MACHINERY

sewing machine with ⅛" (3 mm) gauge foot

GETTING STARTED

- Before making your belt, you need to make a test strip, or mini-belt, to ensure that your belt will fit your buckle properly. The test strip tests not only the buckle's fit but also the size of the prong slot and the wraparound length. It also gives you a chance to practice sewing, setting any rivets or eyelets, and punching holes. Your test strip should be approximately 6" (15 cm) long, wide enough to accommodate the size of your buckle, and made of the same materials that you'll be using for your finished belt. (continued on next page)

RAW-EDGE-BELT TEST STRIP

GETTING STARTED (continued)

MAKING A TEST STRIP AND KEEPER

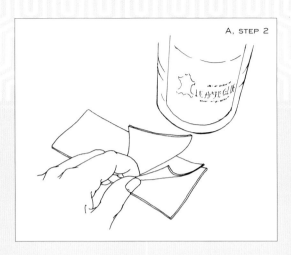

A, STEP 2

STEP 1

Choose a raw-edge belt test-strip pattern from those provided on page 110 to fit a buckle whose width is ³/₄" (2 cm), 1" (2.5 cm), 1¹/₂" (4 cm), or 2" (5 cm); or adjust the pattern to make it ¹/₁₆" (2 mm) narrower than your particular buckle width. Cut a piece of leather, filler, and lining ¹/₂" (1.3 cm) larger all around the pattern.

STEP 2

Rubber-cement the leather, filler, and lining layers together like a sandwich, with the filler layer in the middle. (See illustration A.) Use masking-tape loops on the back of the pattern to stick it on top of the sandwich and keep it in place (be sure to test beforehand to see if

the masking tape takes off the leather's finish; if it does, use pattern weights instead to hold the pattern in place). Cut out the belt with a utility knife, using the edge of the ruler as a guide along the edge of the pattern piece.

STEP 3

If you're using a harness buckle, you'll need a keeper, which will keep the belt tip secure after it goes though the buckle. To make a keeper, cement together a piece of the outside leather and lining leather (you can omit the filler). The width of the keeper is a design element— and your choice as the designer—but its length is determined by the materials the belt is

made of. The keeper must be long enough to wrap fully around the belt and have its ends meet at the back, with enough extra length to allow the belt tip to pass through it comfortably. Cut the keeper to the appropriate length, butt the ends together, and use a pliers stapler to staple the abutted ends. (See illustration B.)

STEP 4

Use the test-strip pattern to mark and punch out the prong slot and rivet holes. The wraparound allowance may also need to be adjusted, depending on the buckle you're using. For instance, you'll need more wraparound length when using a harness buckle and a keeper than when using

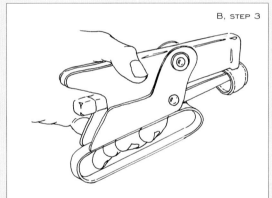

B, STEP 3

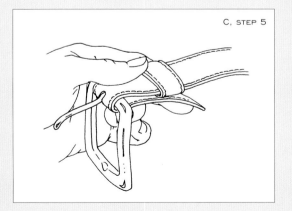

C, STEP 5

a center-bar buckle. Also, use the test strip to be sure that the prong slot is the appropriate width and length to accommodate the belt prong; it should wrap around the prong comfortably, with the base of the prong resting at the end of the slot cut out on both the front and back of the belt. (A thick belt will require a longer prong slot than a thin belt.) If the prong slot is too short, you can lengthen it by moving and punching the oval punch beyond the previously punched oval. Finally, practice sewing and topstitching on the test strip in order to make any needed adjustments to the tension setting on your machine.

INSTRUCTIONS

MAKING A RAW-EDGE BELT

STEP 5

Test the fit of the buckle on the test strip. Practice riveting or stitching the buckle on, but know that you'll need to remove the buckle and use it on your full-length belt. To practice attaching a keeper, rivet or stitch the buckle onto the test strip as close to the buckle as possible. Slide the keeper on the test strip with the stapled ends between the outside and wraparound allowance. (See illustration C.) Rivet or stitch the test strip again on the other side of the keeper to keep it in place.

If the test strip fits the buckle and its wrap-around allowance is correct, you're ready to move on to making the full-length raw-edge belt. If the test strip does not fit properly, make adjustments to the pattern and make a second test strip.

STEP 1

Use your test-strip pattern to make a full-length belt pattern for your desired waist size. Determine the belt's length by inserting the prong into the test-strip pattern's prong slot, then measuring the desired belt length from the buckle's inside bar, and marking where the center hole, also called the "sizing hole" (the hole in which you want to wear the belt), will be. Add length beyond the sizing hole for an equal number of evenly spaced holes on either side of it (there are usually two to four holes surrounding the sizing hole). Finally, add enough length to

the end of the belt so that when it's worn on the last hole, the belt tip still passes through the buckle and keeper, covering where rivets will be placed after the belt is constructed. Make a keeper pattern based on the size made for the test strip and label your patterns "Raw-Edge Belt," noting on them the waist size and positions for all the holes for oval and round punches.

STEP 2

Cut one piece each of the outside, lining, and filler materials to the size noted in the materials list above.

STEP 3

Rubber-cement all three layers together like a sandwich, as you did for the test strip, and cut out the pieces with a metal ruler as a guide on top of the pattern's edge. (If you're making a keeper, rubber-cement the outer leather and lining layers together, but omit the filler layer. Cut the keeper to size.)

STEP 4

Punch out the prong slot and holes as marked on the pattern. At this point, you can use edge dye with a brush or dauber to paint the belt's raw edges if you like. Wipe off any excess dye on the front and back of the belt as you work.

STEP 5

Using the gauge foot on your sewing machine, topstitch all around the edge of the belt and keeper, sewing 1/8" (3 mm) from the edge.

STEP 6

Wrap the belt around the buckle, inserting the prong through the slot.

STEP 7

Rivet the belt together, close to the buckle. *Note: Use one rivet for a narrow belt or two placed side by side for a wider belt.* If you have a keeper, abut the ends and staple them together with the plier stapler. Then slip the keeper onto the belt, sandwiching its stapled ends between the belt and the wraparound allowance. Then rivet the wraparound in place.

TURNED-EDGE
❧ BELT ❧

A turned-edge belt consists of filler (bonded leather) covered by the outer leather or fabric which has an extra (³/₈" [1 cm]) edge that gets turned to the belt's wrong side. A raw-edge lining (made using the same pattern as for the filler) is then glued to the wrong side of the belt. *Note: Even though a turned-edge belt is usually topstitched, doing so is not mandatory. Just remember that if you're topstitching the belt, use rubber cement (which will not gum up your sewing machine); if you're not, use all-purpose cement. In either case, you'll need to make a test strip to ensure that the belt fits properly on the buckle. If you choose to use fabric as your outer material, be sure to use eyelets or grommets after punching holes for closing the belt, which will ensure that the fabric at the holes does not fray (eyelets and grommets can also provide a decorative element).*

MATERIALS

one strip of light- to medium-weight leather or fabric for outside of belt

one strip of light- to medium-weight leather or vinyl for lining of belt

one strip of belt filler material, ideally bonded leather; a firm, thin strip of scrap leather can be substituted

rubber cement

masking tape (or pattern weights)

one center-bar or harness buckle

one to four rivets (one or two for center-bar buckle, depending on width of belt; two to four for harness buckle); length of rivet posts should just fit through thickness of belt doubled over onto itself

thread for machine sewing

eyelets or grommets if making fabric belt; optional for leather belts. *Note: Be sure that opening of eyelets or grommets accommodates size of buckle prong.*

TOOLS

long piece of pattern paper (thick, manila-type paper works best)

utility or craft knife

awl

scissors

rotary or handheld hole punch, size #1 (³/₃₂" [2.5 mm]) for rivets

oblong punch (size should fit buckle prong)

48" (122 cm) metal ruler

12" (30.5 cm) metal ruler

bone folder

rivet-setting kit

plier stapler

rawhide mallet or hammer

long cutting mat

cardboard or thick leather to place under belt when using handheld punches

eyelet- or grommet-setting kit (if using eyelets or grommets)

MACHINERY

sewing machine with ¹/₈" (3 mm) gauge foot

GETTING STARTED

MAKING A TEST STRIP

STEP 1

Choose a turned-edge-belt test strip pattern from those provided on page 111 to fit a buckle whose width is ³/₄" (2 cm), 1" (2.5 cm), 1¹/₂" (4 cm), or 2" (5 cm); or adjust the pattern to make it ¹/₈" (3 mm) narrower than your particular buckle width to allow for extra bulk of the turned edge. Cut pieces of the outside leather, filler, and lining following the pattern labels.

STEP 2

Apply rubber cement to the filler and the wrong side of the outer material and let the cement dry. Then adhere the filler to the wrong side of the outer material, centering the filler. Cement the wrong side of the outer material's edge, let the cement dry, and turn the edge over the filler using the bone folder.

STEP 3

Apply cement to the wrong side of the lining and the filler side of the outside/filler piece and let the cement dry. Then adhere the lining to the wrong side of the outside/filler piece, centering it.

STEP 4

Follow steps 4 and 5 for making a raw-edge-belt test strip on page 22. As a general rule, when making a keeper for a turned-edge belt, your keeper should also have a turned edge. Likewise, if your belt is topstitched, your keeper should be topstitched as well. Make sure that the leather and the filler for your keeper are not so thick that the edges can't be turned under neatly (if they can't be, choose a thinner leather or a thinner filler, or both). If the test strip fits the buckle, has the correct wraparound allowance, and so on, continue to make the full-length turned-edge belt. If the test strip does not fit properly, make adjustments to the pattern and make a second test strip.

TURNED-EDGE BELT TEST STRIP

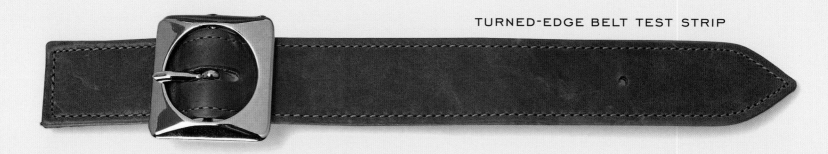

INSTRUCTIONS

MAKING A TURNED-EDGE BELT

STEP 1

Use the test-strip patterns to make full-length patterns for a turned-edge belt in your desired waist size. Follow step 1 from the Raw-Edge Belt instructions on page 23 to determine the length and sizing hole to be labeled on the lining/filler pattern. Make a keeper pattern based on the size made for the test strip, label your patterns as "Turned-Edge Belt," and note on them the waist size and all oval and round punch holes.

STEP 2

Cut one piece of each of the outside, filler, and lining materials following the pattern labels.

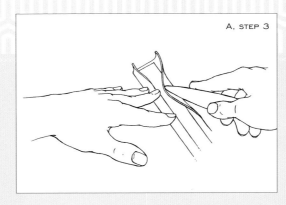

A, STEP 3

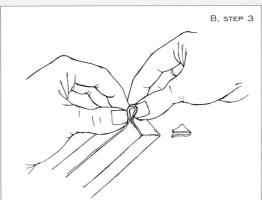

B, STEP 3

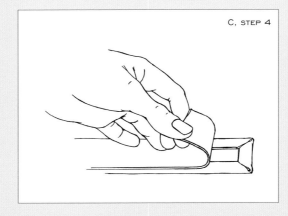

C, STEP 4

STEP 3

To construct the belt, first cement the filler to the wrong side of the outer material. Cement the wrong side of the outer material's edge all around and turn the edge over the filler strip, just as you did on the test strip. Pinch and trim the excess at the corners. (See illustrations A and B.)

STEP 4

Cement the lining to the wrong side of the belt. (See illustration C.) Topstitch all around the belt 1/8" (3 mm) from its edge and punch the holes and attach the buckle, as you did on the test strip. If you're attaching eyelets or grommets to the belt holes, do so at this point. Then finish the belt as described in steps 6 and 7 of the instructions for the Raw-Edge Belt on page 23.

CHAPTER 2

QUICK-AND-EASY, NO- AND LOW-SEW PROJECTS

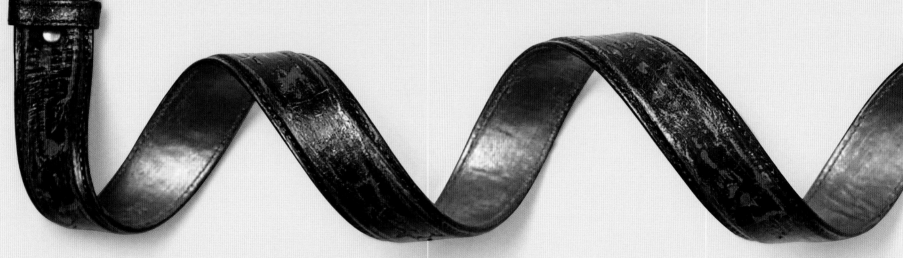

QUICK-DISTRESS
❧ BELT ❧

MATERIALS

one ready-made belt (or make
   your own)

two different colors of acrylic or
   leather paint

metallic-finish gold-leaf wax
   (we used Rub 'n Buff)

crackle medium for acrylic paint
   (like Plaid Folk Art)

water-based sealer
   (for example, Mod Podge)

TOOLS

paintbrush

sandpaper

soft cloth

Here's the perfect way to alter the appearance of a relatively boring, ready-made belt by adding color and texture without a lot of work. We've taken a basic store-bought belt and distressed it to give it an antique, more rugged finish. This is a great project for moms-on-the-go or for your favorite "troupe" of kids. A belt with this type of finish also makes a great Father's Day gift for the outdoorsman in your life.

INSTRUCTIONS

STEP 1

Paint the belt with the desired color of acrylic or leather paint. This will be the color seen coming through the crackles. Let the paint dry.

STEP 2

Following manufacturer's instructions, apply a coat of the crackle medium and let the coat dry.

STEP 3

Paint the belt with a top coat of the second color of acrylic or leather paint. (See illustration A.) Be sure to apply this coat thinly, or it will not crackle well. Let the coat dry, and the paint should start to crackle and allow the color underneath to show through. If you want the belt to appear more distressed, use sandpaper to gently rough up the surface.

A, STEP 3

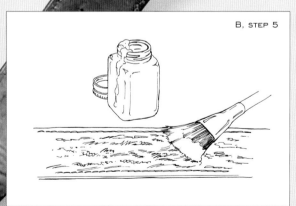

B, STEP 5

STEP 4

Apply the metallic-finish gold-leaf wax sparingly with a soft cloth. Don't completely cover the paint effects; just add highlights to raised areas and edges.

STEP 5

Apply one to two coats of the water-based sealer, allowing it to dry between coats. (See illustration B.) If any paint has gotten on the buckle or hardware, it will peel off easily once dry.

CANDY STRIPER
❦ BELT ❧

MATERIALS

one ready-made belt with a double- or triple-prong buckle and rows of two or three prong holes extending the length of the belt. If you can't find a belt like this, choose a plain belt with a double- or triple-prong buckle and punch your own hole, or just make the belt from scratch.

a bunch of your favorite candy wrappers (enough to thread one through each row of holes)

acrylic or leather paint

water-based sealer (we used Mod Podge)

grommets with washers (grommet size should be big enough for buckle prong to fit through opening and deeper than belt's thickness but not so big that grommets overlap when set through belt holes). Number of grommets needed depends on how many different sizes you want belt to adjust to and number of prongs in your buckle (we had a triple-prong buckle and wanted belt to adjust to three different sizes, so we needed nine sets of grommets).

one strip of thin leather (or vinyl) for lining, cut to same width as belt with its length extending ½" (1.3 cm) beyond the belt's first and last holes

permanent contact adhesive (such as Petronio's All-Purpose Cement)

¼" (6 mm) double-sided craft tape

TOOLS

paintbrush

rawhide mallet or hammer

handheld hole punch (size to accommodate grommets)

needle-nose pliers

grommet-setting kit

8-oz. leather or ¼" to ½" (6 mm–1.3 cm) wood for punching board

If you have a sweet tooth for the extraordinary, this candy-wrapper belt will make your mouth water! This is a store-bought belt, enhanced with candy wrappers and grommets. Paint the belt to change its color or to match a particular outfit. Whatever you decide, this belt will be eye candy for your wardrobe. (The type of ready-made belt needed can often be found at a bargain street-vendor's stall or at discount and dollar stores. Be sure to look for a belt with prong holes along its entire length that are *not* strengthened with grommets.)

INSTRUCTIONS

STEP 1

Paint both sides of the belt with your desired color of acrylic or leather paint and allow the paint to dry. Apply a second coat, if the belt needs further coverage, and allow this coat to dry. (If you get paint on the buckle, it will peel off easily once dry.)

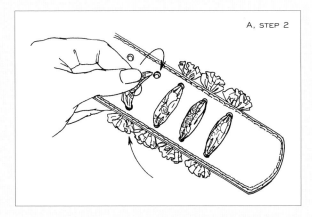

A, STEP 2

STEP 2

Feed a candy wrapper through each line of holes using the needle-nose pliers. Starting from the back of the belt, insert one end of the wrappers in the top hole so it exits on the front of the belt, then feed the wrapper into the bottom hole so it exits on back. (See illustration A.) Adjust each wrapper so that its ends flare nicely and you're pleased with how each "stripe" looks.

STEP 3

Apply double-sided tape along the top and bottom edges of the lining side of the belt to anchor the ends of the candy wrappers in place.

STEP 4

Apply a layer of the contact adhesive to the lining side of the belt through the section with the candy wrappers, extending ½" (1.3 cm) lengthwise beyond the first and last lines of holes (over the entire surface where the belt lining will be attached). Next, apply contact adhesive to the wrong side of the leather strip of belt-lining material. Allow the adhesive on both surfaces to dry, then attach the lining to the inside of the belt.

STEP 5

Apply a thin layer of the water-based sealer to the entire belt, front and back, including the ends of the candy wrappers (but excluding the buckle). Allow the sealer to dry. Apply one or two additional coats of sealer, allowing the sealer to dry after each application.

STEP 6

Decide where you want to position three lines of belt-prong holes to make the belt's size adjustable and punch holes with the handheld punch through the candy wrappers and belt (line up the grommet holes with the existing holes in the belt).

STEP 7

Using a grommet-setting kit, set grommets through the punched holes.

LACE IT UP!
❧ BELT ❧

MATERIALS

one store-bought belt made of single
 layer of leather or vinyl

¹⁄₈" (3 mm) flat lacing, natural color
 (length = 6 × belt's length)

¹⁄₈" (3 mm) flat lacing, medium brown
 (length = 6 × belt's length)

TOOLS

one single-prong lacing punch

one four-prong lacing punch

two lacing needles

awl

metal ruler (the longer the better—
 48" [122 cm] is ideal)

rawhide mallet or hammer

8-oz. leather or ¹⁄₄" to ¹⁄₂" (6 mm–1.3 cm)
 wood for punching board

GETTING STARTED

- The store-bought belt
 used for this project
 had a decorative line
 along the edge that was
 followed for punching
 the lacing holes. If your
 belt does not have
 a similar line, use a
 metal ruler and an awl
 to scratch a guideline
 along the edge of the
 belt ¹⁄₄" (6 mm) away
 from the edge.

Remember those old belts that you have hanging in the back of your closet? Well, take them out, dust them off, and get lacing! That's right. By adding decorative stitching to the edge of a store-bought belt, you're not only altering the overall appearance of the belt but also updating it with fashion and style.

INSTRUCTIONS

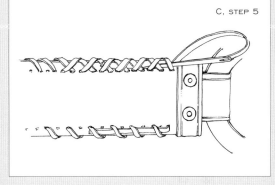

A, STEP 2

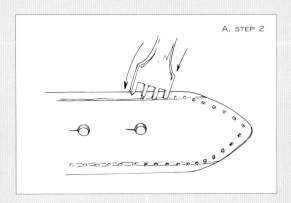

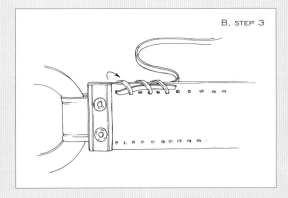

B, STEP 3

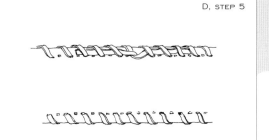

C, STEP 5

D, STEP 5

STEP 1

Use the single-prong punch to punch the holes around the tip of the belt, spacing them like the prongs on the four-prong punch. (Always use a punching board under the belt to protect the table or surface on which you're working.)

STEP 2

Use the four-prong punch to make holes following the line along the belt's straight edge. To maintain even spacing, place the first prong of the four-prong punch in the last hole punched. This means that you'll be punching three holes at a time. Punch holes all the way around the belt's edge. (See illustration A.)

STEP 3

Thread one end of the lacing into the lacing needle and begin at the hole closest to the buckle. Leave a 1½" (4 cm) tail to secure the lacing under the first four stitches. (See illustration B.)

STEP 4

Whipstitch over the belt's edge though every other punched hole all the way around the belt. When you reach the end of the belt, thread the lacing's tail under the last four stitches to secure the end.

STEP 5

Begin whipstitching with the second color of lacing where you ended with the first. Thread the lacing's tail under the first four stitches and stitch through every other hole that was left open, creating a cross-stitch pattern of the two colors. (See illustration C.)

Finish the end by threading the lacing's tail under the stitches in the back of the belt. *Note: If the lacing breaks as you're stitching, begin stitching with a new piece of lacing by threading the new end under the stitches on the back of the belt.* (See illustration D.)

SHIPS-AHOY-AND-AFLOAT
WEBBED BELTS

As you know, belts are not just for women. Here we offer two very easy belts for men made from cotton webbing, one more nautical and the other camouflage-patterned. These are so easy to make that you can conceivably craft a dozen while watching *Oprah!* Surprise the man in your life with a whole collection of these one-of-a-kind beauties.

MATERIALS

For Metal Military-Buckle Belt

48" (122 cm) (or waist size plus 8" [20.5 cm]) of 1¼" (3 cm) webbing

one 1¼" (3 cm) metal military buckle and metal tip

For Plastic Side-Release-Buckle Belt

48" (122 cm) (or waist size plus 8" [20.5 cm]) of 1" (2.5 cm) webbing

one 1" (2.5 cm) plastic adjustable, side-release buckle

two child-size elastic-band hair ties (to use as keepers)

Note: If the webbing design is two-sided, the belt can be easily reversed.

INSTRUCTIONS

METAL MILITARY-BUCKLE BELT

STEP 1
Open the buckle's "teeth," insert the webbing, and manually fold the teeth back down to grip the webbing.

STEP 2
Place the metal tip over the other end of the webbing and manually squeeze the tip closed to finish this end of the belt.

PLASTIC SIDE-RELEASE-BUCKLE BELT

STEP 1
Thread one end of the webbing through each end of the buckle so the excess webbing is on the inside of the belt.

STEP 2
Cut each of the webbing's loose ends to 3" to 5" (7.5–12.5 cm) so they're even.

STEP 3
Slip the elastic-band keepers over the loose ends to secure them for a neat finish.

MOTHER-DAUGHTER REVERSIBLE
⊰ RIBBON BELTS ⊱

MATERIALS

For Mother's Belt

48" (122 cm) of 3" (7.5 cm) ribbon in color/
pattern A

48" (122 cm) of 3" (7.5 cm) ribbon in color/
pattern B

one 2" (5 cm) center-bar buckle (without a
prong)

thread to match

For Daughter's Belt

24" (61 cm) of $^3/_4$" (2 cm) ribbon in color/
pattern A

24" (61 cm) of $^3/_4$" (2 cm) ribbon in color/
pattern B

two $^3/_4$" (2 cm) D-rings

thread to match

TOOLS

home sewing machine with zipper foot

iron

hand-sewing needle

double-stick tape or straight pins

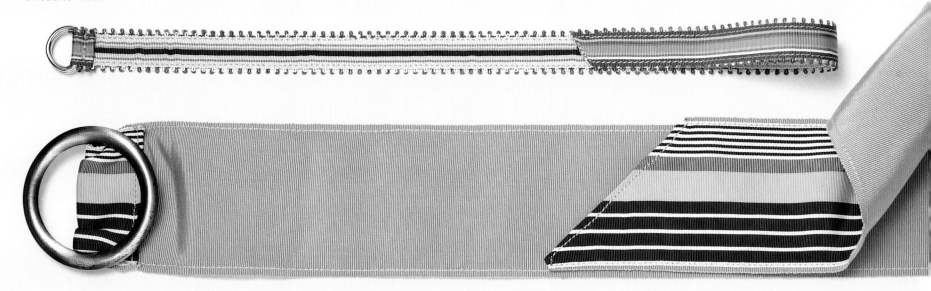

What little girl doesn't want to play dress up with her mother's clothes, and what mother doesn't want to accommodate her daughter's request? Our mother-daughter ribbon belts are a wonderful way to do both.

Ribbons are so much fun these days because they come both in a variety of widths and also in exciting patterns, colors, and styles. These belts are so simple to construct, you may want to make one for every day of the week.

GETTING STARTED

- Iron the ribbon flat, using the appropriate heat setting on your iron for the ribbon's fiber content.

INSTRUCTIONS

STEP 1

Cut one end of all four ribbons with a straight edge. Cut the other end of each ribbon at a 45-degree angle, making the angled cut on each pair of coordinating ribbons mirror one another. Fold over ¼" (6 mm) at both ends of all four pieces of ribbons and use double-stick tape, straight pins, or an iron to secure the fold. (See illustration A.)

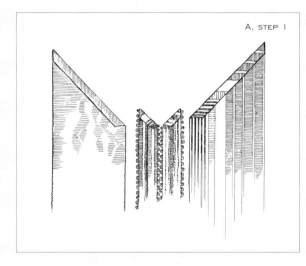

A, STEP I

STEP 2

Placing the two sides of each belt wrong sides together (with the folded edges facing one another) and aligning all the edges, use double-stick tape or straight pins to anchor the sides in place.

STEP 3

Topstitch around all four sides of each belt about ⅛" (3 mm) from the edge, backstitching at the beginning and end of the stitching line.

STEP 4

For the daughter's belt, attach the D-rings to the belt by wrapping the belt's straight end around both D-rings and folding the end over ¼" (6 mm) for a neat finish (you may want to pin the fold in place until you

start topstitching). Then replacing your machine's regular foot with your zipper foot and positioning the folded edge facing up, topstitch through the folded edge and belt beneath to secure the folded edge, backstitching at the beginning and end of the stitching line.

For the mother's belt, attach the center-bar buckle by wrapping the belt's straight end around the center bar. Hand-stitch the straight, topstitched edge in place to secure the buckle (because the ribbon is a little wider than the center bar, it will be slightly "gathered" on the center bar).

THROW-ME-A-LINE
⚜ WOVEN BELT ⚜

MATERIALS

48" (122 cm) piece of ¼" (6 mm) polyester boat line in blue

48" (122 cm) piece of ¼" (6 mm) polyester boat line in green

48" (122 cm) piece of ⅛" (3 mm) polyester boat line in yellow

72" (183 cm) piece of ⅛" (3 mm) polyester boat line in green

two 1½" (4 cm) carabineers

instant adhesive (we used Super Glue)

masking tape

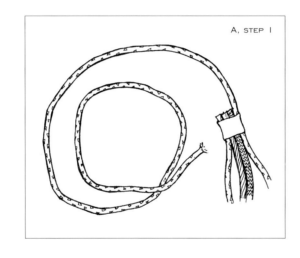

A, STEP I

INSTRUCTIONS

STEP 1

Tape the ends of all four lines together, with an extra 12" (30.5 cm) of the ⅛" (3 mm) green line extending beyond the ends of the other three lines. (See illustration A.)

STEP 2

Begin a four-piece braid as follows:

Separate strands 1 and 2 to the left and strands 3 and 4 to the right.

Pull strand 4 over strand 3, and pull tight. (See illustration B.)

Pull strand 1 over strands 2 and 4, and pull tight. (See illustration C.)

Pull strand 3 over strand 1, and pull tight. (See illustration D.)

Pull strand 2 over 4 and 3, and pull tight. (See illustration E.)

Repeat the process to lengthen the braid.

Do you remember those summers as a kid when you spent time in camp making lanyards? We've given you a more modern version of that time-honored hobby. Using boat cording in a variety of colors, we've created a woven belt that's sure to keep your pants afloat. In keeping with the nautical theme, we've used carabineers as buckles. Attach the carabineers together for a classic look, or slip each one onto the woven part of the belt for another look. Both ways work!

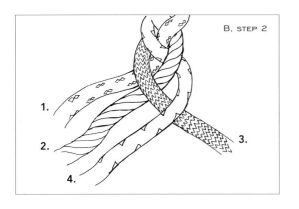

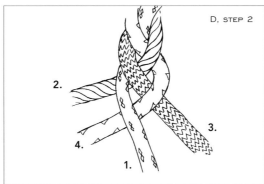

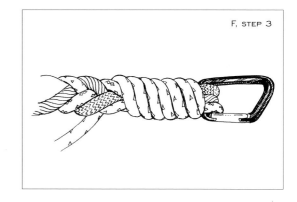

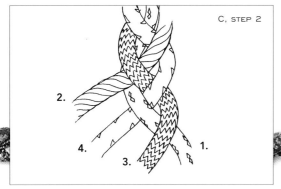

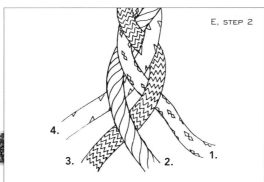

STEP 3

Thread the ends of the boat line through each carabineer. Fold the ends over the carabineer, and wrap the ⅛" (3 mm) green line around the ends to secure the carabineer. Apply instant adhesive as the line is wrapped to strengthen the wrap. Tie the ends of the lines and dab the knot with instant adhesive to ensure that it stays tied. Weave the excess end of the line through the braid and cut off the remaining excess. (See illustration F.)

X MARKS THE SPOT
❧ BELT ❧

This stylish belt makes a wonderful gift for every person in your family or circle of friends. It also makes a perfect project for an after-school group or a Girl Scout troop. Try using felt or vinyl instead of leather for this belt to give it a completely different look. You could also mix and match fabrics or patterns for yet another variation. And don't forget that this belt is perfectly reversible. Whatever your design choices, make sure to mark your spot creatively.

MATERIALS

3" × 30" (7.5 × 76 cm) piece of 3- to 4-oz. leather in rose

3" × 24" (7.5 × 61 cm) piece of 3- to 4-oz. leather in olive

4 yards (3.7 m) of round leather lacing cut into two 2-yard (1.8 m) pieces

TOOLS

rotary or handheld hole punch, size ³/₃₂" (2.4 mm)

scissors

utility or craft knife

leather-marking pen

instant adhesive (we used Super Glue)

small cutting mat

8-oz. leather or ¼" to ½" (6 mm–1.3 cm) wood for punching board

patterns (see page 123)

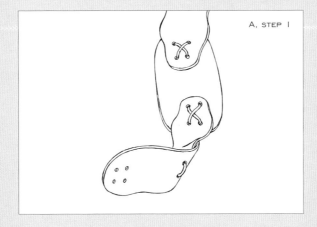

A, STEP 1

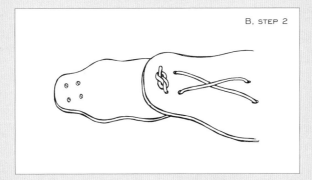

B, STEP 2

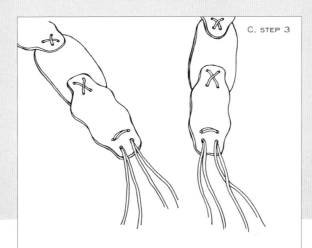

C, STEP 3

GETTING STARTED

• Cut out all the leather pieces using the two patterns, following the cutting directions on the patterns. Cut around each pattern piece with a utility knife, or trace the pattern and cut the tracing with scissors. Punch all holes with a rotary punch or a handheld hole punch.

Pull the lacing's two ends through the holes. (See illustration A.)

STEP 2

Lace in and out of the holes to form an "X" pattern in the overlapping ends of the two pieces. Continue to add, overlap, and lace new sections just as you did with the first pair. When you reach the last overlapping holes, tie off the ends of the lacing and add a dab of instant adhesive to ensure that the knot stays tied. (See illustration B.)

INSTRUCTIONS

STEP 1

Use 2 yards (1.8 m) of round leather lacing to lace the pieces together as follows: Begin by overlapping one Section A piece over one Section B piece and aligning the lacing holes in one end. Thread each end of one piece of lacing from the back through the first two overlapping holes.

STEP 3

Cut the remaining 2 yards (1.8 m) of lacing into four equal pieces. Lace two pieces through the four holes at each end of the belt, as shown, to create the belt's tie. (See illustration C.)

SLIT-PLAITED
❧ BELT ❧

MATERIALS

one 36" × 1½" (91.5 × 4 cm) piece of medium-weight black leather, such as cowhide (for approximate size 32" [81.5 cm] belt; use a larger or smaller piece, depending on desired belt size)

one 35" × 1½" (89 × 4 cm) piece of medium-weight white leather, such as cowhide (likewise, adjust size of piece depending on desired belt size)

one 1" (2.5 cm) center-bar buckle

two ¼" (6 mm) -long rivets

permanent contact cement (such as Petronio's All-Purpose Cement)

black leather or acrylic paint with paintbrush (optional)

TOOLS

1" (2.5 cm) oblong punch

rotary or handheld hole punch, size #1 (³/₃₂" [2.5 mm])

rivet-setting kit

utility or craft knife

long metal ruler (36" to 45" [91.5–114.5 cm] is ideal)

rawhide mallet or hammer

masking tape or pattern weights

long cutting mat

cardboard or thick leather for punching board

patterns (see page 113)

GETTING STARTED

- Cut the leather strips for the interlacing belts and the belt tip from the two patterns as labeled. Use loops of masking tape to hold the patterns in place on the leather (check first on a leather scrap to see if the masking tape takes the finish off your leather; if it does, use pattern weights to hold down the patterns instead). Line up the metal ruler along the straight edge of each pattern, and cut the pattern pieces with a utility knife.

This quick and easy belt is just the right accessory for jeans as well as a suit. It can be made for both men and women in a variety of colors and fabrics. You can alter the size of the plaits to suit your mood or enhance a special outfit. Plaiting, the technique used for this belt, which is sometimes referred to as braiding, was very popular in the 1960s and involves interlacing strands of leather (or another material). Because the retro look is very popular nowadays, we've added a more fashionable look to the classic silhouette.

INSTRUCTIONS

STEP 1

Use the oval punch and rawhide mallet to punch oval punches along the length of the belt strips, as marked on the patterns. (See illustration A.) Then use the rotary or handheld hole punch to punch holes for rivets, as marked on the patterns.

STEP 2

Starting at the buckle end, with the black strip on top, weave the black strip down through the first oval punch in the white strip (leave the first oval punch in the black strip free for attaching the buckle later). Then weave the white strip down through the second oval punch in the black strip. Keep alternately weaving the black and white strips through each other until you get to the end of the belt. (See illustration B.)

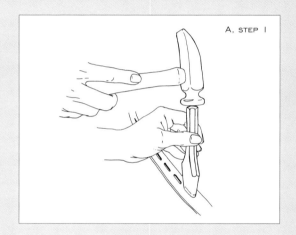

A, STEP I

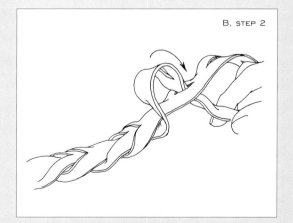

B, STEP 2

STEP 3

Attach the buckle to the starting end of the belt by looping the black strip's first oval punch around the buckle's center bar and prong, sandwiching the end of the white strip between. Line up all the rivet holes on this end and set a rivet through all three layers using the rivet-setting kit.

STEP 4

Cement the wrong side of the black belt tip to the right side of the white belt tip using all-purpose adhesive. Then cement the separate black tip to the wrong side of the white belt tip. Make sure all the rivet holes are lined up and set a rivet through all three layers using the rivet-setting kit. If desired, paint the edge of the belt tip with the leather/acrylic paint.

JUST ZIP IT!
❧ BELT ❧

Simple and *fun* are two apt words to describe this belt. Made from a zipper and bound on either side with leather, this belt can be worn with jeans or over a skirt in various ways to suit your whim. Add your favorite zipper pull (ours is an earring), and you have a versatile, one-of-a-kind fashion statement.

MATERIALS

25" (63.5 cm) #10 metal-tooth zipper and pull

60" (152.5 cm) piece of ³/₄" (2 cm) premade leather binding

one size-24 snap set

thread to match for machine- and hand-sewing

TOOLS

snap-setting kit

glover's needle

double-stick tape

scissors

rotary or handheld hole punch, size ¹/₈" (3 mm)

8-oz. leather or ¹/₄" to ¹/₂" (6 mm–1.3 cm) wood for punching board

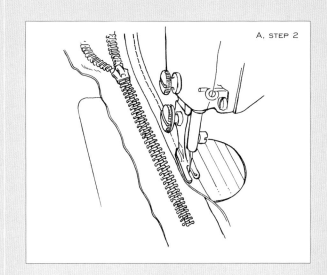

A, STEP 2

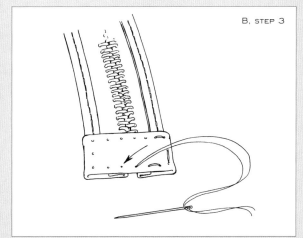

B, STEP 3

INSTRUCTIONS

STEP 1

Use double-stick tape to fold and secure the leather binding evenly over each of the zipper's two long cloth edges.

STEP 2

Topstitch the binding on the zipper ¹/₈" (3 mm) away from the bound edge. (See illustration A.)

STEP 3

To reduce bulk at both ends of the zipper, carefully cut away the metal teeth along the last ¹/₂" (1.3 cm) of each side of the zipper, leaving the cloth intact. Use double-stick tape to cover the closed end of the zipper with a 3³/₄" (9.5 cm)

piece of leather binding. Machine- or hand-stitch (using a glover's needle) the binding to the zipper tape. (See illustration B.)

STEP 4

Use double-stick tape to cover the zipper's two open ends with two 3" (7.5 cm) pieces of leather binding. Machine- or hand-stitch (using a glover's needle) the binding over the zipper tape on each open end. Punch a hole in the center of each leather-bound open end and set a snap through the two holes, with the male set on one side and the female set on the other.

CHAPTER 3
❧ CLASSIC BELTS ❧
WITH CREATIVE
VARIATIONS

"PICTURE THIS!"
❧ BELT ❧

MATERIALS

two 42½" × 3" (108 × 7.5 cm) strips of medium-weight black leather, such as cowhide (for a size 36" [91.5 cm] belt; you may use a longer or shorter piece, depending on desired belt size)

one 7" × 5½" (18 × 14 cm) piece of thin black leather for lining belt buckle

one 5" × 5½" (12.5 × 14 cm) piece of thick cardboard (approximately ¹/₁₆" [2 mm] thick)

one 5" × 5½" (12.5 × 14 cm) piece of thin cardboard (approximately ¹/₃₂" [1 mm] thick)

one 5" × 5½" (12.5 × 14 cm) piece of felt or Pellon

fabric sheets for inkjet printers (such as Printed Treasures by Milliken); you can also use iron-on T-shirt transfer sheets for inkjet printers, or find a local print shop that can print photo images on fabric

¼" (6 mm) -wide double-sided craft tape

one screw post/collar button/collar stud

one 2" (5 cm) rectangular ring or D-ring

ten ¼" (6 mm) -long rivets

rubber cement

Fray Check by Dritz

thread for machine sewing

TOOLS

rotary or handheld hole punch, size #1 (³/₃₂" [2.5 mm]) for rivets and screw post, and size #6 (³/₁₆" [5 mm]) for belt holes

four-in-one punch (we used Craftool brand; it punches four ³/₃₂" [2.5 mm] holes side-by-side at once), or use a single ³/₃₂" [2.5 mm] hole punch

rivet-setting kit

long metal ruler (36"–45" [91.5–114.5 cm] is ideal)

12" (30.5 cm) metal ruler

scissors

utility or craft knife

awl

What a great way to show off photos of your friends and family, your last vacation, or your favorite urban landscape, as we did on our version of this belt. Our belt features scrapbook-style photos in a whole new way. Wear your pictures on your hips for a guaranteed photo-finish outfit!

bone folder

flathead screwdriver

rawhide mallet or hammer

masking tape or pattern weights

fabric-marking pencil

felt-tipped pen

long cutting mat

cardboard or leather for punching board

patterns (see pages 114–115)

MACHINERY

home sewing machine with adjustable-gauge foot

computer with imaging software

inkjet printer

GETTING STARTED

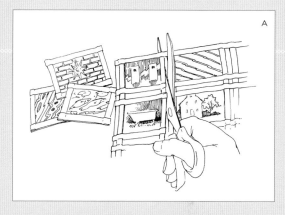

A

- Choose the pictures you want to use for your belt. We used seventeen pictures for a size 36" (91.5 cm) belt plus one photo for the buckle; adjust the number used for the belt length you want.

- Resize the pictures on your computer so they each measure 2¹/₈" × 1⁷/₈" (5.5 × 4.5 cm). Lay out the pictures for each 8¹/₂" × 11" (21.5 × 28 cm) sheet to be printed so there's a minimum of at least ¹/₂" (1.3 cm) border around each picture. Resize the picture for the buckle so that it measures 3¹/₄" × 2¹/₈" (8.5 × 5.3 cm), and leave at least a ³/₄" (2 cm) border around this image.

- Print the pictures on fabric sheets designed for inkjet printers or on iron-on transfer sheets, following the manufacturer's instructions for the product you use.

- Adhere ¹/₄" (6 mm) double-sided craft tape around each edge of the smaller belt pictures printed on fabric (but don't peel the backing off the tape yet). Trim around the outer edge of the tape with scissors for each picture. (See illustration A.)

- Use a fabric-marking pencil to draw a border ³/₄" (2 cm) away from the edge of the printed picture to be used for the buckle and cut out the image along the marked border.

- Trace the buckle pattern on felt or Pellon with a felt-tipped pen and cut it out.

- Use the utility knife to cut all the leather and cardboard pieces for the belt from the patterns as labeled, except for the belt lining (keep the original 42¹/₂" × 3" [108 × 7.5 cm] leather-lining strip intact for now). Use loops of masking tape to hold the patterns in place on the leather (check beforehand to make sure that the tape doesn't take the finish off the leather; if it does, use pattern weights instead). Line up the metal ruler along the straight edges of the patterns and cut around the patterns with a knife. To cut out the "windows" on the outside-leather belt, transfer a pin mark in each corner of each window with the awl, remove the pattern, connect the pin marks with a ruler, and cut out the windows with the utility knife.

INSTRUCTIONS

MAKING THE PHOTO BUCKLE

STEP 1

Using rubber cement, attach the belt-buckle lining leather to the thin cardboard lining, carefully centering the lining on the leather. With the lining side up, glue the leather's outer edges to the underside of the cardboard, using the bone folder to turn the edges over the cardboard neatly. Pinch the excess leather at each corner together and trim it with scissors so it resembles a mitered corner on a picture frame. Transfer the rivet and screw-post hole placements onto the buckle lining piece by pushing through the pattern with the awl onto the leather. Punch out the marked holes with the size #1 hole punch. Transfer and punch the holes from the leather Tab for Ring pattern onto the cut piece.

STEP 2

To attach the ring to the buckle lining, first match up the tab to the lining so that the holes line up. Set the first two rivets with the rivet-setting kit, slip the ring between the two layers, and then set the last two rivets. Screw in the screw post so that its knob faces the finished side of the lining. (See illustration B.)

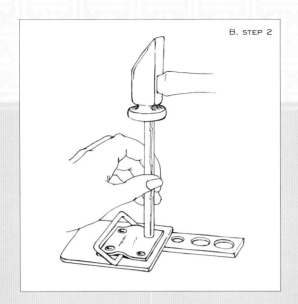

B, STEP 2

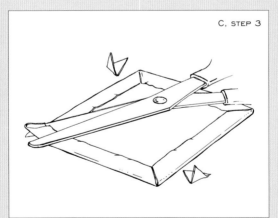

C, STEP 3

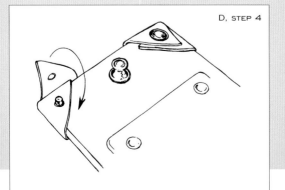

D, STEP 4

STEP 3

Attach the cut felt or Pellon to the thick cardboard buckle piece with double-sided tape. Place the printed fabric piece for the buckle face down on the table; center the felt-lined cardboard piece on top of it, felt-side facing down; and glue the outer edge of the fabric onto the cardboard side of buckle with rubber cement. Use the bone folder to turn in the edges all around over the cardboard. Pinch and clip away the excess fabric at the corners as you did for the leather on the belt buckle. (See illustration C.) *Note: Be careful to center the image so that it has an even ³/₈" (1 cm) border around it. Also be sure not to glue the felt directly on the back of the fabric because the glued fabric/felt unit will dent when any pressure is placed on the buckle; instead, glue only the fabric's outer edges. Rubber-cement the buckle front and the buckle's lining pieces together.*

STEP 4

Transfer and punch the rivet holes in all four corners of the buckle. Transfer and punch the holes in each "photo corner." Fold the leather corner pieces over the corners of the buckle so that the ends overlap each other in back, then set the rivets through each corner using the rivet-setting kit. (See illustration D.)

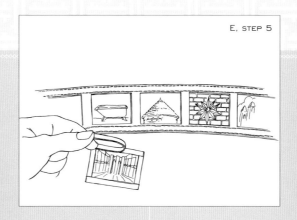

E, STEP 5

MAKING THE "PICTURE" BELT

STEP 5

Peel off the double-stick tape from the fabric mini-pictures. Adhere them to the underside of the leather cut for the outer belt, centering them so that they show through the cut-out windows. (See illustration E.) *Note: Be sure that the images face the correct direction according to which side you placed the screw post in your buckle, so that your buckle and belt pictures both face the same way.*

STEP 6

Rubber-cement the outer belt to the belt lining piece (the lining should be larger than the belt at this point). Using the gauge foot on your machine, topstitch all around the belt $^{1}/_{16}$" (2 mm) from the outer belt's edge. Trim the excess lining away with scissors so that the edges of the lining and belt are flush.

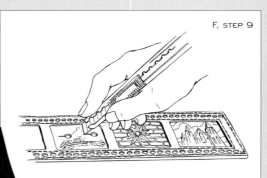

F, STEP 9

STEP 7

Using the gauge foot, sew a second row of top-stitching all around the belt at $^{5}/_{16}$" (8 mm) from the edge.

STEP 8

Punch a series of tiny decorative holes along the belt's top and bottom edges using the four-in-one punch and centering the holes' placement between the two topstitching lines. Before punching the holes, it may help to use the awl and ruler to scratch a faint line on your leather through what will be the center of the holes in order to line up the holes evenly.

STEP 9

Transfer and punch the size #6 ($^{3}/_{16}$" [5 mm]) holes in the belt as marked on the pattern. Use a knife to cut a tiny slit in each hole on the side closest to the buckle in order to allow for the screw post to fit snugly through the belt when worn. (See illustration F.) Carefully apply Fray-Check on the inner edges of the holes to prevent fraying.

STEP 10

To attach the buckle, first transfer and punch the four rivet holes at the end of the belt. Wrap the end of the belt around the ring on the buckle, match up the rivet holes, and set the two rivets to secure the buckle.

GATHERED CINCH
❧ **BELT** ❧

This cinch belt made from gathered fabric is striking and sensational. Wear it with a simple black dress to create a sophisticated, feminine silhouette, or make it out of Scotch plaid and wear it over a flowing, long blouse or layered Ts to top off a pair of jeans. The belt is accentuated with oversized, silver-finish hook-and-eye closures.

MATERIALS

one wide piece of elastic cut to your waist size; elastic will slightly overlap at center on finished belt (our elastic was 29" [73.5 cm] long × 3½" [9 cm] wide for a 29" [73.5 cm] size belt)

one piece of fabric (or very thin vinyl/leather) 3" (7.5 cm) longer and 2" (5 cm) wider than elastic

three 1½" (4 cm) -wide hook-and-eye closures (or use a larger number of smaller sets, if preferred)

thread for machine and hand sewing

TOOLS

scissors

straight pins (or ½" [1.3 cm] binder clips if using leather/vinyl)

hand-sewing needle

ruler or tape measure

fabric-marking pen

MACHINERY

home sewing machine with zigzag capability

presser foot and zigzag foot for machine

INSTRUCTIONS

STEP 1

Using straight pins (or binder clips), pin the long edges of the fabric (or vinyl/leather) to the long edges of the elastic, with right sides facing each other and leaving 3/8" (1 cm) of fabric extending beyond the elastic's edge on the long sides and 1 1/2" (4 cm) extra fabric extending beyond each short end of the elastic. Stretch the elastic as you pin the fabric to it to create gathers. To ensure evenly distributing the gathers, start pinning the fabric to the elastic at both ends first, then pin at the center, then at the center of each half, and so on.

STEP 2

With the elastic side facing up and using a straight stitch on your sewing machine, sew the elastic to the fabric along the long sides only. Sew as close to the edge of the elastic as you can and stretch the elastic as you sew. Be sure to backstitch at the beginning and end of each row to lock the stitches to prevent raveling. Remove the straight pins. When you've sewn the top and bottom edges together, you will have a long, gathered tube.

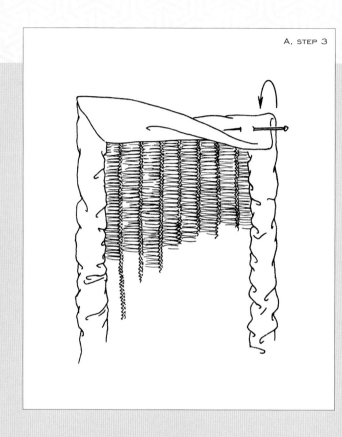

A, STEP 3

STEP 3

Turn the belt right side out through one of the open ends. Double-fold the remaining 1 1/2" (4 cm) of extra fabric at the top and bottom edges of the belt, pinning or clipping the folded edges in place. Then double-fold each short end onto itself, so that a 3/4" (2 cm) folded edge is visible on the underside of the belt, similarly pinning or clipping the folded edges in place. (See illustration A.) Then zigzag-stitch down each short end to secure the folded ends, about 1/2" (1.3 cm) in from the edge.

STEP 4

Adjust the extra fabric at the top and bottom of the belt's long edges so it's evenly distributed and pin it in place. With the belt's right side up, zigzag-stitch down the center of the belt along its length. Starting at one end, stretch the elastic as you sew to the other end, backstitching at the beginning and end of the stitching line. (See illustration B.)

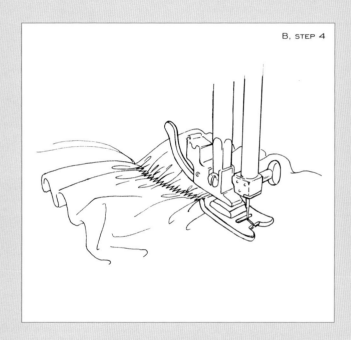

B, STEP 4

C, STEP 5

STEP 5

Hand-sew the hook-and-eye closures to the ends of belt, spacing the pairs evenly. To ensure a correct fit, hold the belt in place on yourself to position the hooks and eyes before sewing them on. (See illustration C.)

TABLECLOTH-SASH
❧ **BELT** ❧

I'm sure that some of you will remember the episode of the old *I Love Lucy* TV show in which Lucy and Ethel dress up in clothes made out of old tablecloths. Well, we've taken that concept to a whole new level.

Our tablecloth-sash belt is high-fashion and fabulous. Made of vinyl checkered tablecloth material and sporting a handmade flower buckle, this belt is sure to have everyone asking for seconds!

MATERIALS

two long strips of vinyl checkered tablecloth material (we used two pieces 40³/₄" × 6³/₄" [103.5 × 17 cm] for a size 32" [81.5 cm] belt)

two 5" (12.5 cm) squares of soft, thin leather (or vinyl)

one 5" (12.5 cm) square of thick cardboard (about ³/₃₂" [2.5 mm] thick)

one 5¹/₂" (14 cm) -long piece of 1¹/₄" (3 cm) -wide grosgrain ribbon

two ¹/₄" (6 mm) -long rivets

one 3" (7.5 cm) square of craft foam

permanent contact cement (such as Petronio's All-Purpose Cement)

contrasting thread for machine sewing

matching thread for hand sewing

leather or acrylic paint (to match buckle)

TOOLS

rotary or handheld hole punch, size #1 (³/₃₂" [2.5 mm])

rivet-setting kit

scissors

utility or craft knife

bone folder

binder clips

hand-sewing needle

masking tape

fabric-marking pencil

fine paintbrush

small cutting mat

rawhide mallet or hammer

8-oz. leather or ¹/₄" to ¹/₂" (6 mm–1.3 cm) wood for punching board

patterns (see page 112)

MACHINERY

home sewing machine with adjustable-gauge foot

INSTRUCTIONS

MAKING FLOWER BUCKLE

STEP 1

Cut the cardboard, leather, and craft-foam pattern pieces using the flower-buckle patterns (as labeled). For the cardboard and leather, use loops of masking tape on the back of the pattern to adhere it to the cardboard and the right side of the leather (be sure to test beforehand to make sure that the masking tape does not take the finish off the leather; if it does, trace the pattern on the leather's right side instead. Place your work on a cutting mat and cut around the pattern carefully with a utility knife. For the craft foam, cut "trapunto" flower pieces by tracing the pattern onto the foam and cutting it out with scissors.

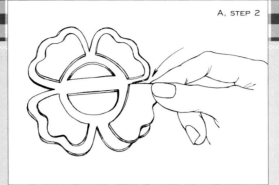

A, STEP 2

STEP 2

Attach the four craft-foam trapunto pieces to the cardboard buckle by applying contact cement to both surfaces. Allow the cement to dry, then attach one craft-foam piece in the center of each petal. (See illustration A.)

STEP 3

Apply contact cement to the craft-foam side of the cardboard buckle, the trapunto foam pieces, and the wrong side of the outside leather. Let the cement dry, and adhere the cardboard to the leather's wrong side, centering it on the leather. Using the bone folder on the leather's right side, define the trapunto relief all around the edges of the craft foam. (See illustration B.)

STEP 4

Flip the buckle over so that its wrong side faces you. Cement the entire surface of the cardboard and leather "turn-in allowance," and allow the cement to dry. Using the bone folder, crease and pleat the leather as needed all around the outer edges of the flower to get the allowance to turn in cleanly. When you get to a "corner" between petals, cut a slit through the leather (as marked on pattern) in order to make it conform to the cardboard's shape. Be sure not to cut too far into the leather, or the cardboard will show through. Try to turn and press the leather all around the edges of the flower with the bone folder, pressing hard to adhere the edges

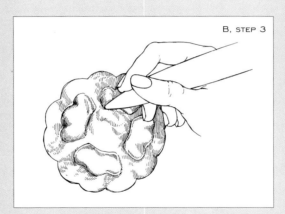

B, STEP 3

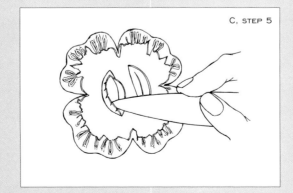

C, STEP 5

(this will be a bit difficult, but take your time and be patient). After you've pressed down the edges as best as you can, use the utility knife to cut away the excess pleated leather, trying to make the surface as smooth as possible. After cutting away the excess, rub the turned edges with the bone folder to flatten the leather.

STEP 5

Cut slits through the buckle's leather center, as marked on the pattern (again, be careful not to cut too close to the corner or the cardboard will show). Fold the cut leather onto

the cardboard with the bone folder and flatten it down as you did for the outer edge. (See illustration C.) Apply contact cement to the entire wrong side of the buckle and to the wrong side of the leather lining. Allow both surfaces to dry, then adhere them together carefully. Rub the bone folder firmly over the surface to attach the pieces securely.

STEP 6

Using the paint and brush, touch up the edges of the buckle where any raw edges of leather or cardboard show through.

MAKING THE SASH BELT

STEP 7

Cut two long strips of vinyl checkered tablecloth material about 9" (23 cm) longer than your desired belt size and 6¾" (17 cm) wide (6" [15 cm] plus a ⅜" [1 cm] seam allowance on top and bottom) with the checks laid out diagonally across the belt. Cut the belt tip to a point, using the checkered motif as a guide and leaving a ⅜" (1 cm) seam allowance around the entire tip, and cut the end to be attached to the buckle straight.

STEP 8

Using binder clips, clip the two cut pieces together all around the edges, with the right sides facing each other.

STEP 9

Sew all around the edge of the belt with a ⅜" (1 cm) seam allowance, leaving a 6" (15 cm) -wide opening at the belt's center bottom edge for turning the belt to the right side. Clip the excess bulk away from the seam allowance at each corner and turn the belt right side out.

STEP 10

Making sure the seam allowances at the opening are folded under and using the adjustable-gauge foot on your machine, top-stitch two rows around the entire edge of the belt, with the first row ⅛" (3 mm) from the edge and the second row ½" (1.3 cm) from the edge.

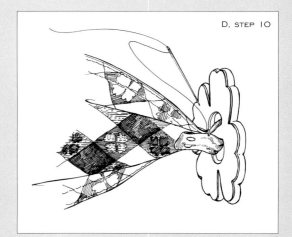

D, STEP 10

ATTACHING THE BUCKLE

STEP 11

Fold under each end of the 5½" (14 cm) strip of ribbon by ¾" (2 cm), and then fold the ribbon in half, wrong sides together, so that its length now measures about 2" (5 cm). Feed the folded ribbon around the flower buckle's center bar so that both folded ends are on the buckle's wrong side.

STEP 12

Make a box pleat at the straight end of the belt so that it fits within the ribbon's width. Encase the end of the belt between the two ribbon ends and punch two holes (one at each corner of the ribbon) through all layers with the hole punch. Set rivets to attach the buckle, using the rivet-setting kit (it will be easier to do this on the edge of a table so that the buckle is not in the way). Finally, hand-sew a tack stitch on each side of the ribbon close to the buckle in order to firmly secure the buckle. (See illustration D.)

REVERSIBLE-LINK
❧ BELT ❧

Can't decide which belt to wear with your outfit? Don't worry. This reversible-link belt will fit your ever-changing lifestyle. If you want simplicity, go with a one-color link all around; but if you want to liven up this project, be creative in making—and wearing—this belt by alternating the leather colors and/or the sizes of the links. To alternate the side of the link that shows when you wear the belt, you'll use a small screwdriver to remove the screw-in studs that hold the belt closed, then rearrange the links and replace the stud closure. However you choose to wear this belt, it will surely get noticed.

MATERIALS

Note: We used ten links to make an approximate size 36" (91.5 cm) belt. Depending on your desired belt size, you may need more or less leather and more or fewer rivets.

two pieces of leather, each a different color, measuring 30" × 22" (76 × 56 cm)

double-capped rivets; length of rivet post should just fit through thickness of both layers of leather (we used three different size caps: 80 large, 78 medium, and 80 small)

two screw-in studs/collar buttons

one 2" to 3" (5–7.5 cm) O-ring

edge dye or leather/acrylic paint

permanent contact adhesive (such as Petronio's All-Purpose Cement)

masking tape or pattern weights

TOOLS

rotary or handheld hole punch, size #1 ($^3/_{32}$" [2.5 mm])

12" (30.5 cm) metal ruler

rivet-setting kit

utility or craft knife

awl

small screwdriver

paintbrush, cotton swab, or dauber for applying edge dye

rawhide mallet or hammer

small cutting mat

cardboard or thick leather to place under belt if using handheld punches

patterns (see pages 116–117)

INSTRUCTIONS

STEP 1

Using the all-purpose adhesive, completely coat the wrong sides of both pieces of leather. Allow both surfaces to dry, then adhere them together.

STEP 2

Use loops of masking tape on the back of the patterns to stick them on top of the cemented leather (test the masking tape beforehand on the leather to make sure that it doesn't take off the leather's finish; if it does, hold the patterns in place with pattern weights). Cut out the links as directed in the pattern labels, using a sharp knife and the edge of the ruler as a guide on top of the pattern's edge. When cutting the rounded corners, simply use the edge of the pattern as a guide. *Note: Be sure to keep the knife at a right angle to the cutting surface. It may be easier to cut the leather into smaller, more manageable pieces before cutting the actual pattern pieces.*

STEP 3

Apply the edge dye or paint to the raw edges of all the links and allow the paint to dry.

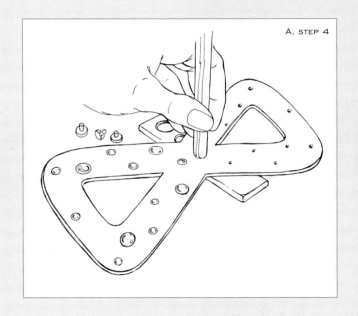

A, STEP 4

STEP 4

Transfer all the markings for rivets and screw-in studs to the cut pieces with the awl, as marked on the patterns. Punch all the holes as marked, using the rotary or handheld punch. On the last link, make slits on the two holes of the extended tab with a knife, as marked on the pattern. Set rivets through all the holes except the two on the last link, which are reserved for the screw-in studs. (See illustration A.)

Note: We set the different-size rivet caps in a pattern on this belt to give it an interesting visual "texture." Since the rivet holes marked on the pattern are all the same size, regardless of the size of the rivet cap you use, you can set up your own pattern with the different-size rivets and use it consistently throughout the belt.

STEP 5

"Link" the belt together by threading the first link through the O-ring and folding the link in half. Loop the next link through the openings of the folded link and fold that one in half. (See illustration B.) Repeat this process until you get to the last link with the extended tab.

STEP 6

Loop the last link with the tab through the previous link, fold it in half, and screw the two studs through both layers of the folded link. (See illustration C.) Close the belt by looping the tab through the O-ring and attaching the last holes over the studs.

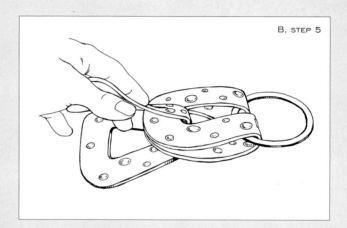

B, STEP 5

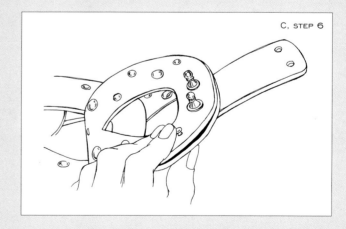

C, STEP 6

PLEATED OBI
❧ BELT ❧

An obi is a sash-like belt originally worn by Japanese women to hold the kimono in place. Our obi is highly stylized and embellished with pleats and beading (the beads are optional but add real drama). This type of belt can be used to dress up any outfit and is also the perfect complement to a simple pair of black slacks for an after-five look. The key is in finding a wonderful patterned fabric.

MATERIALS

one 18" × 10" (45.5 × 25.5 cm) piece of fabric for outside of belt (we used a satin print)

½ yard (45.5 cm) of fabric for belt lining and French binding

one 18" (45.5 cm) -square piece of medium-weight fusible interfacing

2½ yards (228.5 cm) of $2^3/_4$" (7 cm) -wide satin ribbon

assorted beads (we used seed, bugle, and roundel beads)

thread for hand sewing

TOOLS

scissors

beading needle

bone folder

straight pins

binder clips

fabric-marking pencil

iron

patterns (see pages 118–119)

MACHINERY

home sewing machine with presser foot and ⅛" (3 mm) gauge foot

GETTING STARTED

- Cut all fabric and interfacing pieces by tracing the patterns with a fabric-marking pencil and cutting out the pattern pieces with scissors. Iron both of the fusible interfacing pieces to their corresponding fabric pieces, one to the wrong side of the outside fabric and one to the wrong side of the lining fabric. Also, cut two 1½" (4 cm) -wide strips of lining fabric on the bias (cut diagonally across the fabric's straight grain) for a French binding, one 18½" (47 cm) long and the other 17½" (44.5 cm) long. Cut the length of satin ribbon in half.

INSTRUCTIONS

STEP 1

Pleat the interfaced outside fabric so that the center band forms a box pleat as its top layer then fold the top and bottom sides of this band back and forth like a fan so these pleats descend outwards. Hold the pleats flat, iron them, and then tack them in place. (See illustration A.)

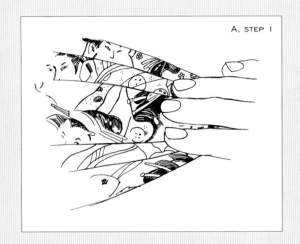

A, STEP I

STEP 2

If you want to embellish your belt with beading, now's the time to do it. Experiment with different beading techniques to find the ones that best accent the design of your outside fabric. We used six simple beading stitches alone and in various combinations: satin stitch, basic running stitch, basic top stitch, dangle stitch, dangle-loop stitch, and vermicelli stitch. (See the sidebar, Beading Techniques.)

BEADING TECHNIQUES

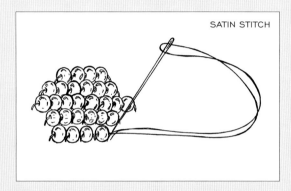

SATIN STITCH

SATIN STITCH: Thread several beads at a time on each running stitch; make closely spaced rows to fill in larger areas.

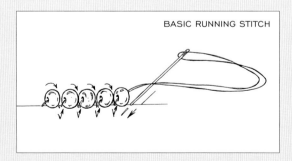

BASIC RUNNING STITCH

BASIC RUNNING STITCH: Bring needle up through right side of fabric, through bead, and then back down through fabric right next to bead; and repeat.

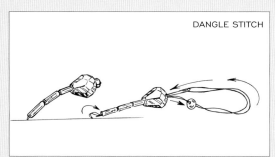

BASIC TOP STITCH

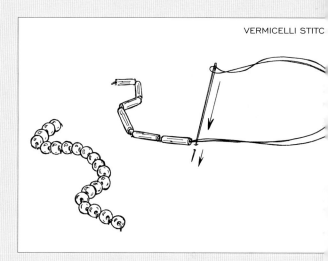

BASIC TOP STITCH: Bring needle up through two beads on right side of fabric; first bead is usually a large one, and second bead, called the "stop," is usually a seed bead. Bring needle back through first bead, then down through fabric to wrong side.

DANGLE STITCH: Bring needle up through several beads on right side of fabric; last "stop" bead is usually a seed bead. Bring needle back through all beads except stop bead, then down through fabric.

VERMICELLI STITCH: As for basic running stitch, bring needle up through right side of fabric, through one or more beads, and then back down through fabric right next to bead, but take each stitch (or several stitches if using small beads) in a different direction to form a zigzag pattern.

DANGLE STITCH

VERMICELLI STITCH

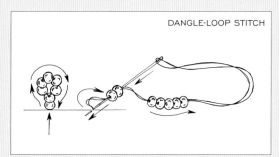

DANGLE-LOOP STITCH

DANGLE-LOOP STITCH: Bring needle up through several beads on right side of fabric; use several beads as the "stop," forming a loop. Bring needle back through first bead, then down through fabric.

INSTRUCTIONS (CONT.)

STEP 3

To sew the French binding to the top and bottom edges of the belt, pin the bias-cut strips of fabric along these edges (the longer strip goes on the top edge), with the right sides of the fabric facing each other and matching up the raw edges. Sew along both edges with a 3/8" (1 cm) -wide seam allowance. Take out the pins and fold binding fabric over the raw edge of the seam allowance to the belt's wrong side, creating a 3/8" (1 cm) -wide bound edge. Hold the turned edges flat using binder clips and iron the turned edges flat in place, removing the clips as you go. (See illustration B.)

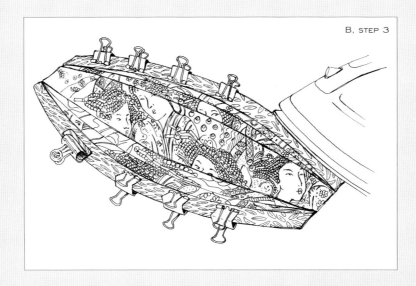

B, STEP 3

STEP 4

Fold the top and bottom edges of the interfaced belt lining to the lining's wrong side, using the edge of the interfacing as a folding guide. Iron the turned edges flat in place.

STEP 5

Sandwich the ribbon ties between the outside and lining layers on each end, with the right sides of the outside and lining layers facing together and the right side of the ribbon facing the outside fabric. Match up the raw edges of the outside layer and lining's short ends with an edge of the ribbon, pleating the ribbon to fit within the width of the belt ends. Hold the assembled end in place with binder clips (See illustration C), and sew each end with a 3/8" (1 cm) -wide seam allowance. After attaching both ribbon ties, turn the belt right-side out and iron the short ends flat.

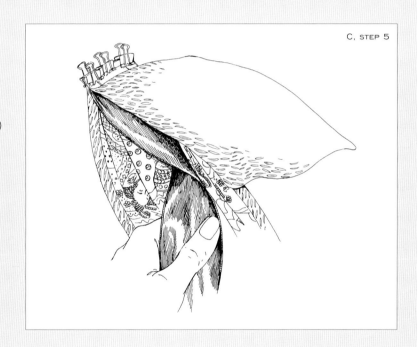

C, STEP 5

STEP 6

Match up the top and bottom edges of the outside belt with the lining and hold them in place with binder clips. Topstitch along the top and bottom edges of the belt using the 1/8" (3 mm) gauge foot to finish the belt.

TARTAN TIME
❧ BELT ❧

What better way to dress up a simple black dress than with our Tartan Time Belt? Made of tartan plaid fabric and trimmed with leather, our belt is sure to make all the other lads and lassies a bit envious.

MATERIALS

¼ yard (23 cm) of outside fabric

¼ yard (23 cm) of lining fabric

1¾" × 36" (4.5 × 91.5 cm) piece of 1- to 2-oz. leather

1" × 36" (2.5 × 91.5 cm) piece of stiff interfacing or belt filler

one 1" (2.5 cm) buckle clip

two size-24 snap sets

rubber cement

matching thread for machine sewing

TOOLS

rotary or handheld hole punch, size ⅛" (3 mm)

straight pins

scissors

utility or craft knife

rawhide mallet or hammer

awl

iron

snap setter

double-stick tape

small cutting mat

8 oz. leather or ¼" to ½" (6 mm–1.3 cm) wood for punching board

patterns (see pages 120-121)

MACHINERY

home sewing machine with adjustable-gauge foot

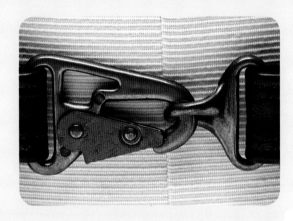

GETTING STARTED

- Cut out all the pattern pieces according to the pattern labels. *Note: Cut the fabric on the bias at a* *45-degree angle to the fabric's straight grain, which runs parallel to the fabric's two selvage edges.*

INSTRUCTIONS

STEP 1

Pin the outside and lining fabric together with the right sides facing each other and the raw edges aligned. Stitch around the pinned shapes, using a $3/8$" (1 cm) -wide seam allowance and leaving a 4" (10 cm) -long opening at the center bottom edge. (See illustration A.)

STEP 2

Turn the belt right side out and press the seam with an iron, folding in and pressing the seam allowances at the 4" (10 cm) opening. Hand-stitch the opening closed.

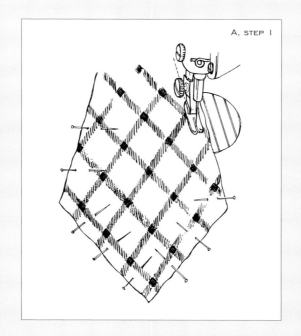

A, STEP 1

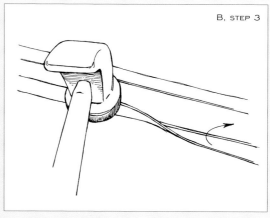

B, STEP 3

STEP 3

Apply rubber cement to the strip of interfacing and to the wrong side of the leather strip. Allow the cement to dry, then adhere the interfacing down the center of the wrong side of the leather strip. Cement the edges of the leather's wrong side and fold them over the interfacing. Hammer the fold if the leather does not fold easily. (See illustration B.)

STEP 4

Topstitch along both edges of the leather strip ¼" (6 mm) away from the edge of the leather.

STEP 5

Use double-stick tape to secure the leather belt evenly down the center of the fabric belt. Topstitch all along both edges of the leather belt ⅛" (3 mm) away from the edge of the leather. (See illustration C.)

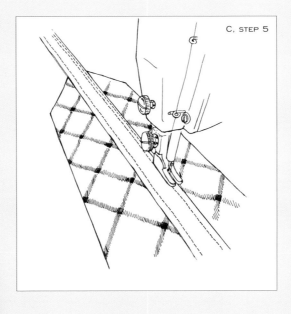

C, STEP 5

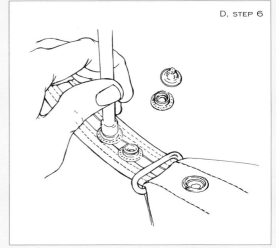

D, STEP 6

STEP 6

Punch holes for the snaps as noted on the pattern labels. Set the two female snap-assembly sets through the leather and fabric.

Thread the buckle pieces onto the leather tips and set the four male snap-assembly sets through the leather tips. (See illustration D.)

BRACE YOURSELF
SUSPENDERS

Braces, or suspenders, have always been a staple in a man's wardrobe, but it was not until World War II that women began to wear them as both a utilitarian and purely fashionable accessory. The pinup girls of the silver screen wore suspenders with everything from skirts to hot pants. Our suspenders feature a slip connector, whose size you can vary and whose location you can vary each time you wear them. Use your imagination in making the connector and create a flower, heart, or animal connector to tickle your fancy. Also, don't just limit yourself to leather; cotton webbing, vinyl, or fabric work well too.

MATERIALS

3" × 48" (7.5 × 122 cm) pieces of outside leather (we used snakeskin)

3" × 48" (7.5 × 122 cm) piece of lining leather (3–4 oz. thick)

four collar pins/screw posts

four ³/₄" (2 cm) suspender clips

rubber cement

matching thread for machine sewing

leather or acrylic paint to dye edge

TOOLS

rotary or handheld hole punch, size ¹/₈" (3 mm)

³/₄" (2 cm) oval punch

scissors

utility or craft knife

metal ruler (24", 36", or 48" [61, 91.5, or 122 cm])

rawhide mallet or hammer

masking tape

fine paintbrush

small cutting mat

8 oz. leather or ¹/₄" to ¹/₂" (6 mm–1.3 cm) wood for punching board

patterns (see page 123)

MACHINERY

home sewing machine with adjustable-gauge foot

INSTRUCTIONS

STEP 1

Using rubber cement, coat the wrong side of both pieces of leather, let the cement dry, and then adhere the pieces together.

STEP 2

Make masking-tape loops and put them on the back of the patterns to keep them in place on the leather (always test beforehand to make sure that the masking tape doesn't take off the leather's finish; if it does, use pattern weights instead). Use a metal ruler and a utility knife to cut through both layers of leather all around the strap and strap-connector patterns. (See illustration A.)

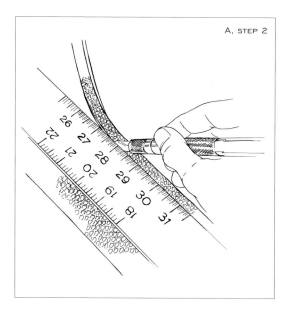

A, STEP 2

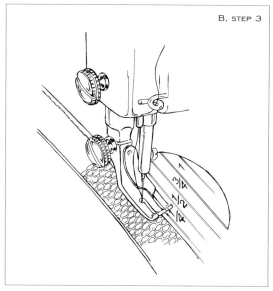

B, STEP 3

STEP 3

Topstitch all around the straps and the strap connector 1/8" (3 mm) away from the leather's edge, using the 1/8" (3 mm) gauge foot. (See illustration B.)

STEP 4

Use the ³/₄" (2 cm) oval punch at the points marked on the pattern to create the two slots for the straps to pass through on the strap connector. (See illustration C.)

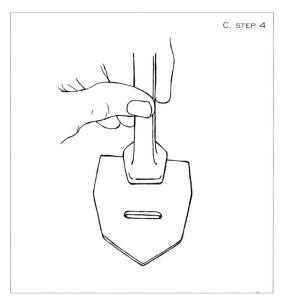

STEP 5

Dye the edge of all the cut pieces with the leather or acrylic paint and a fine paintbrush.

STEP 6

Thread the straps through the strap connector. Punch ¹/₈" (3 mm) holes and cut keyholes in the strap ends as labeled on the pattern. Put the suspender clips onto the straps, making sure they face in the correct direction. Attach all four collar pins to the ends of the straps and secure the strap ends. (See illustration D.)

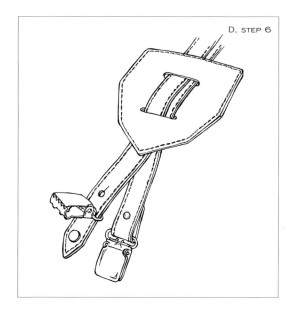

"Where have all the flowers gone?" Onto our Flower Power belt, of course! Check out our bouquet of handmade leather flowers strung on a leather cord with tassel ends. Make as many or as few flowers as you want for this belt. Whether it's flowers by the bunch or just a few special blooms, this belt is sure to put the power in your outfit. While making your belt, why not make a few more flowers and turn them into a bracelet or headband to match your belt?

MATERIALS

1 square foot (0.1 sq. m) of kidskin leather in dark blue

1 square foot (0.1 sq. m) of kidskin leather in medium blue

1 square foot (0.1 sq. m) of kidskin leather in light blue

1 square foot (0.1 sq. m) of kidskin leather in dark yellow

1 square foot (0.1 sq. m) of kidskin leather in light yellow

60" (152.5 cm) length of leather lacing

rubber cement

matching heavy thread for hand sewing

TOOLS

glover's needle

scissors

utility or craft knife

awl

masking tape

small cutting mat

patterns (see page 122)

GETTING STARTED

- Cut all the flower pattern pieces according to the pattern labels. Use a utility knife and cut around the edge of the pattern or trace the pattern onto the right side of the leather and use sharp scissors to cut out the pieces.

INSTRUCTIONS

STEP 1

Transfer the center slit lines from the pattern for Petal A onto the leather pieces with an awl and cut the slits with a utility knife. (See illustration A.)

STEP 2

Rubber-cement the solid edge of the flower-center tassel. Once the cement is dry, roll the tassel onto itself.

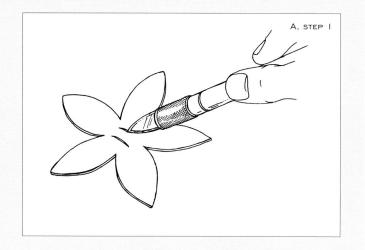

A, STEP 1

B, STEP 3

STEP 3

Stack the petals for one flower, with Petal A on the bottom and petals B, C, D, and the tassel on top. Hand-stitch from the right side of Petal A (to hide the thread's knot) taking a small stitch just to one side of the cut center slit and then take one stitch up through the center of all the petal pieces and the tassel's base. Next stitch back down through the center of all the pieces. Make several more stitches this way, making sure not to stitch the Petal A slits closed. Tie off the thread between petals A and B. When stitching through the tassel, be sure to insert the needle through its solid section. (See illustration B.)

STEP 4

Thread each flower onto the leather lace through the slits in Petal A. Secure the flowers to the lace if you want them to be fixed in position. (See illustration C.)

C, STEP 4

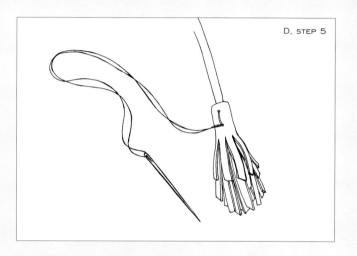

D, STEP 5

STEP 5

Rubber-cement the edge of the lacing-tip tassel and the tips of the lacing. Once the cement is dry, roll the longer strands of each tassel first around each tip of the lacing. Hand-stitch the tassels into place. You can use the awl to make a hole through the tassel and lacing leather to make it easier to sew through if you want. (See illustration D.)

Feast your eyes on this totally original belt-bag version of the Wild West gun holster. Our belt bag features two side pockets perfect for all your valuables. The belt bags fit the contours of your hips for a smooth, not bulky, fit. *Note: You can vary this belt design by eliminating the bag portion from the instructions, leaving only the contoured belt itself.*

MATERIALS

one 40" × 25" (101.5 × 63.5 cm) piece of medium-weight leather, such as cowhide, for outside belt and pockets (for approximate size 32" [81.5 cm] belt; you may use larger or smaller piece, depending on desired belt size)

one 40" × 25" (101.5 × 63.5 cm) piece of medium-weight leather, such as cowhide for belt and pocket lining

two 7" (18 cm) zippers

two 1" (2.5 cm) D-rings

rubber cement

1/4" (6 mm) -wide double-stick craft tape

thread for machine sewing

TOOLS

utility or craft knife

scissors

masking tape or pattern weights

large cutting mat

patterns (see pages 124-126)

MACHINERY

home sewing machine with 1/8"(3 mm) gauge foot

INSTRUCTIONS

STEP 1

Cut out two pieces of leather for the belt and lining approximately 1/2" (1.3 cm) larger all around than the belt pattern. *Note: Be sure to flip the pattern over to the "wrong side" to cut out the lining leather.*

Apply rubber cement to the wrong side of the outside leather and lining pieces. Allow both surfaces to dry, then adhere the two pieces with wrong sides together (and right sides facing out).

INSTRUCTIONS

STEP 2

Using loops of masking tape to hold the patterns in place on the leather (test beforehand to make sure the tape doesn't take the finish off the leather; if it does, use pattern weights instead), cut through both layers using the belt and pocket patterns. (See illustration A.) *Note: Be sure to flip over the pocket pattern to cut out the second pocket.* Use the edge of the patterns as a guide, and cut out the pieces with a utility knife.

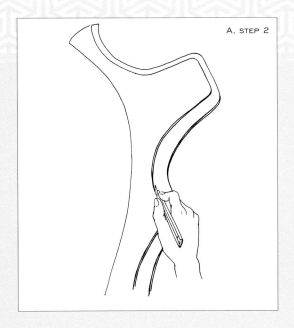

A, STEP 2

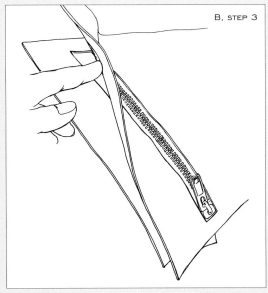

B, STEP 3

STEP 3

On the pocket pieces you cut, cut out the windows for the zippers (as noted on the pattern) and peel apart about ½" (1.3 cm) of the two layers of leather around the window opening so you can insert the zipper between the two layers. Use double-stick tape on both sides of the zipper tape's fabric edges and center the zipper teeth in the window opening (see illustration B), with the zipper pull facing the center front of the belt when closed.

STEP 4

Attach the outer and lining pieces of each pocket back together so that all the edges are lined up, then stitch all around the zipper-window openings using the gauge foot on your machine. Peel back the leather at the outer edges of the short ends of the window, trim any excess zipper tape, then restick the leather back in place.

STEP 5

To stitch each of the two bottom-corner darts on the outer pocket bag, peel apart the layers of the dart's slit edge (marked on the pattern) and sandwich both layers of the dart's inner edge (the one that's notched) between the two layers of the slit edge. Align the sides of the slit edge with the notch on the dart's inner edge. (See illustration C.) Hold the sides of the dart in place with double-stick tape. Topstitch the edge of the dart in place using the gauge foot.

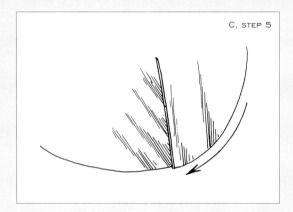

C, STEP 5

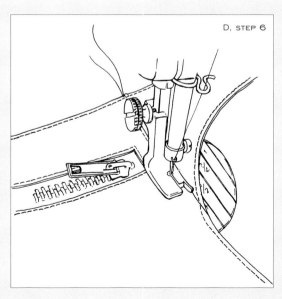

D, STEP 6

STEP 6

Attach each pocket to the outside of the belt by using the double-stick tape along the outer edge of the pocket lining and placing the pocket on the belt so that its outer edge matches up with the belt's outer edge. Using the gauge foot, topstitch all around the outer edge of the belt, attaching the top and bottom parts of the pockets. Next, topstitch the top side sections of the pockets to attach them to the belt as well. Backstitch at the beginning and end of each seam so that there's no visible space between the topstitching on the side edge and the original outer edge. (See illustration D.)

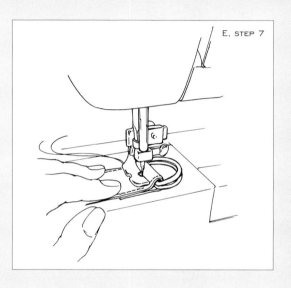

E, STEP 7

STEP 7

Fold the end of the belt around both D-rings (as noted on the pattern) and stitch the end closed using the zipper foot on your machine. Try to stitch as close to the D-rings as possible. (See illustration E.)

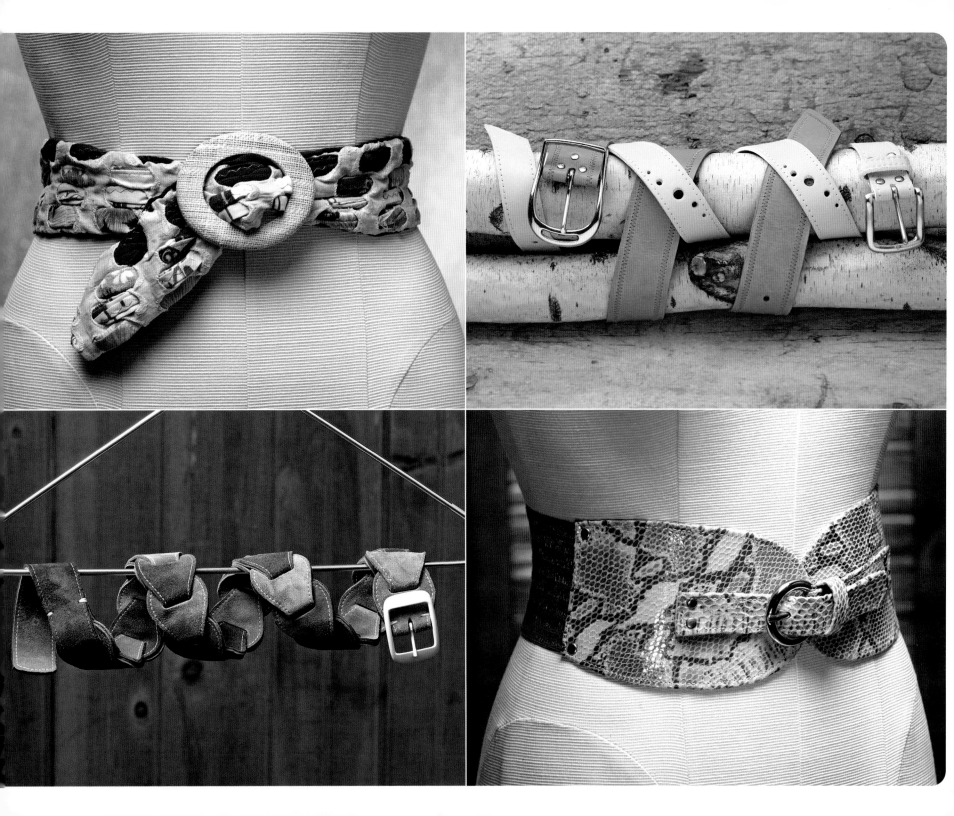

CHAPTER 4

❧ GALLERY ❧

To compile this gallery, we shared our belt patterns with our current class of enthusiastic and talented fashion students at Fashion Institute of Technology (FIT) and invited them to let loose their creative minds. Their assignment was to take the patterns that we had created and change them, modify them, and be as creative as they wanted. The following pages showcase the exciting results. Some of the students took the original patterns and modified the size and changed the fabrics or hardware, while others took the patterns to another level.

And now it is your turn. Use our patterns and the designs of our students as inspiration. Let your mind wander. Check out your drawers and closets for old belts and use the no-sew ideas to bring those belts to life again. Or, use pieces of jewelry, old clothing, or fabric swatches to create something new and one-of-a-kind! With each and every design you create, make sure that your unique personality and talent shine through.

Special thanks to the students from FIT for their interpretations of our patterns and for encouraging all of us to dream!

LEAVES SASH BELT
❧ SONJA HODZODE ❧

INSPIRATION: Tablecloth-Sash Belt

Simple and *elegant* are the two key words to describe this sash belt. The buckle is ivory leather, molded around a dimensional template designed to look like a circle of leaves. This belt is sure to spark the "budding" designer in all of us.

DESPERATE HOUSEWIFE

MONA ALMAZAN

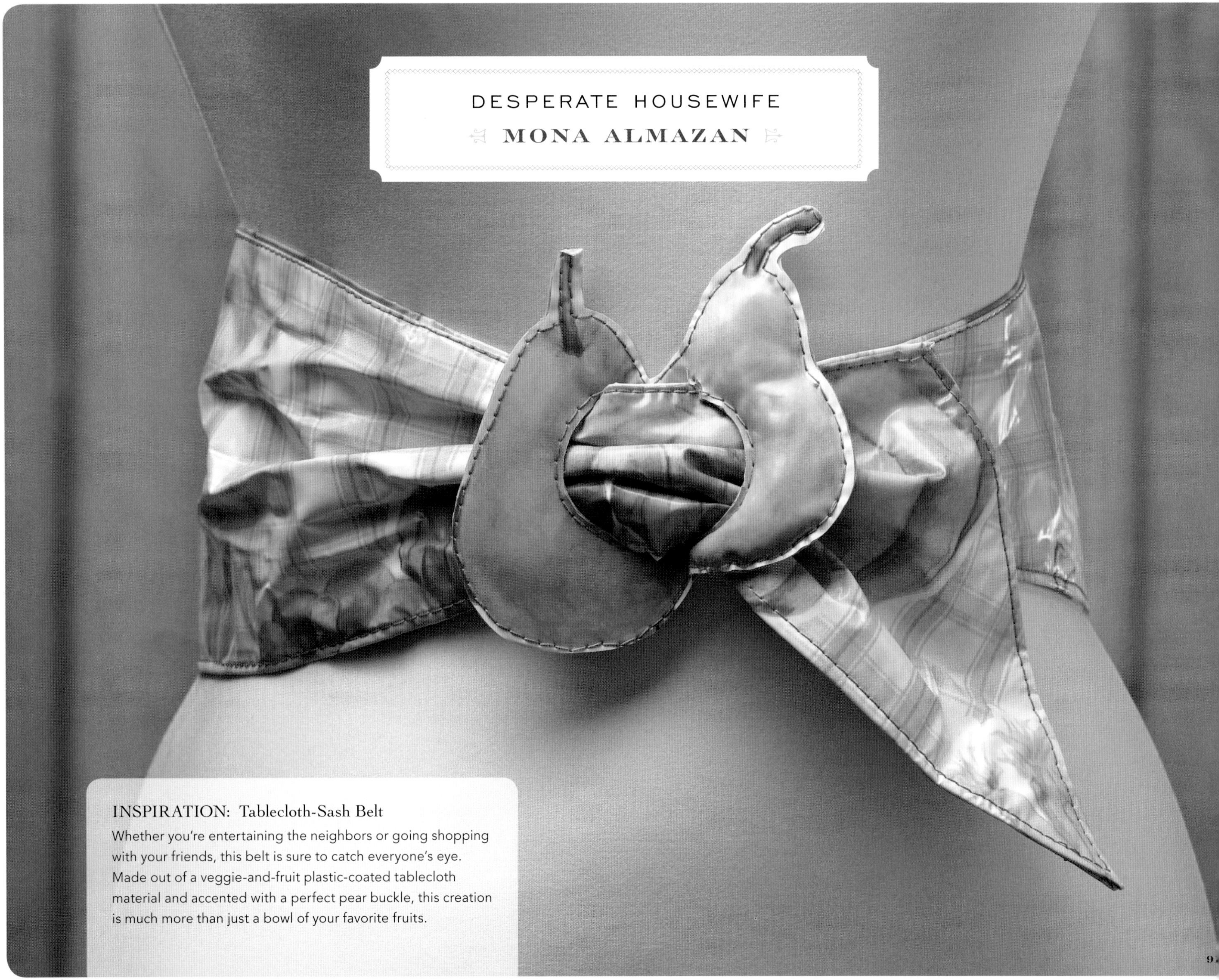

INSPIRATION: Tablecloth-Sash Belt

Whether you're entertaining the neighbors or going shopping with your friends, this belt is sure to catch everyone's eye. Made out of a veggie-and-fruit plastic-coated tablecloth material and accented with a perfect pear buckle, this creation is much more than just a bowl of your favorite fruits.

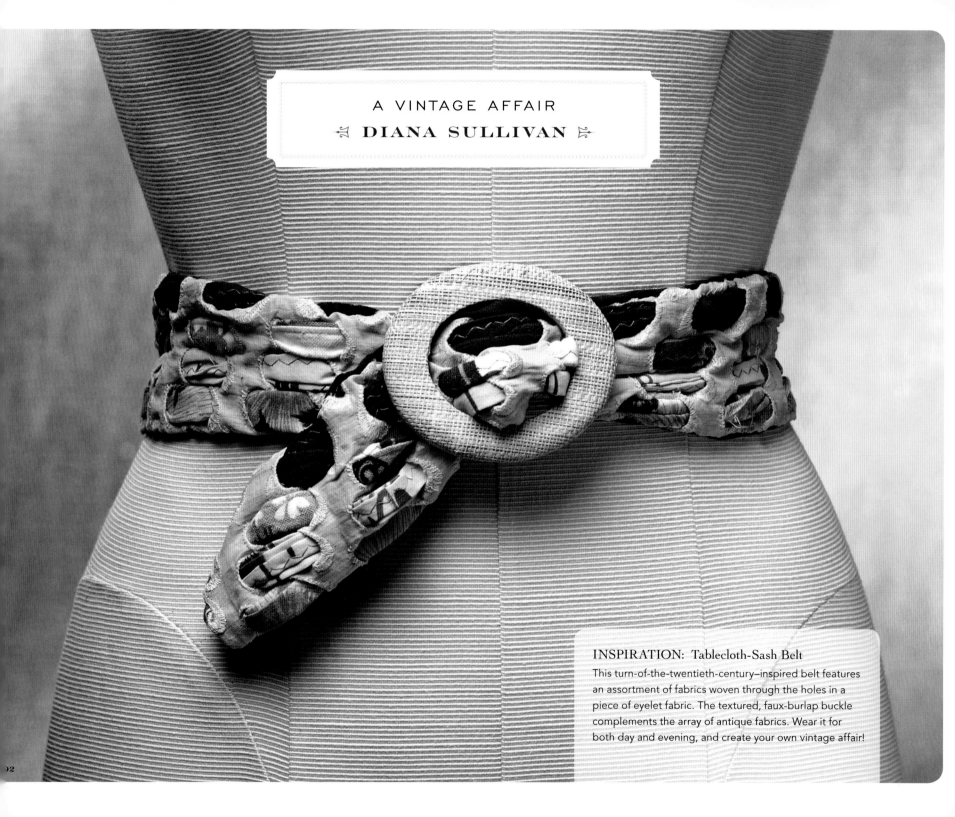

A VINTAGE AFFAIR
❧ DIANA SULLIVAN ❧

INSPIRATION: Tablecloth-Sash Belt
This turn-of-the-twentieth-century–inspired belt features
an assortment of fabrics woven through the holes in a
piece of eyelet fabric. The textured, faux-burlap buckle
complements the array of antique fabrics. Wear it for
both day and evening, and create your own vintage affair!

HANDS-ON
ALLISON DENT

INSPIRATION: Annie-Get-Your-Gun Belt
Whether it's hands-on or hands-off, this variation
of our contour belt bag is sure to make a hit. Made
out of animal print fabric and sporting a pair of
"snap-off" gloves, this belt is an organizer's dream
and an accessorizer's accessory!

RINGING IN THE NEW YEAR
❧ YELENA SIMONTOBOVA ❧

INSPIRATION: Lace It Up! Belt
Bring in the New Year in style with this easy-to-make and highly functional belt. Made of gold rings that are woven together with cotton braid, this belt is sure to feel festive for any glitzy occasion.

INSPIRATION: Reversible-Link Belt

Using multicolored leather links, this contour belt shows off your waist and hips in style. Wear this belt with jeans or a gorgeous black dress and boots for a blast from the past made current! Any way you choose, this belt is a knockout!

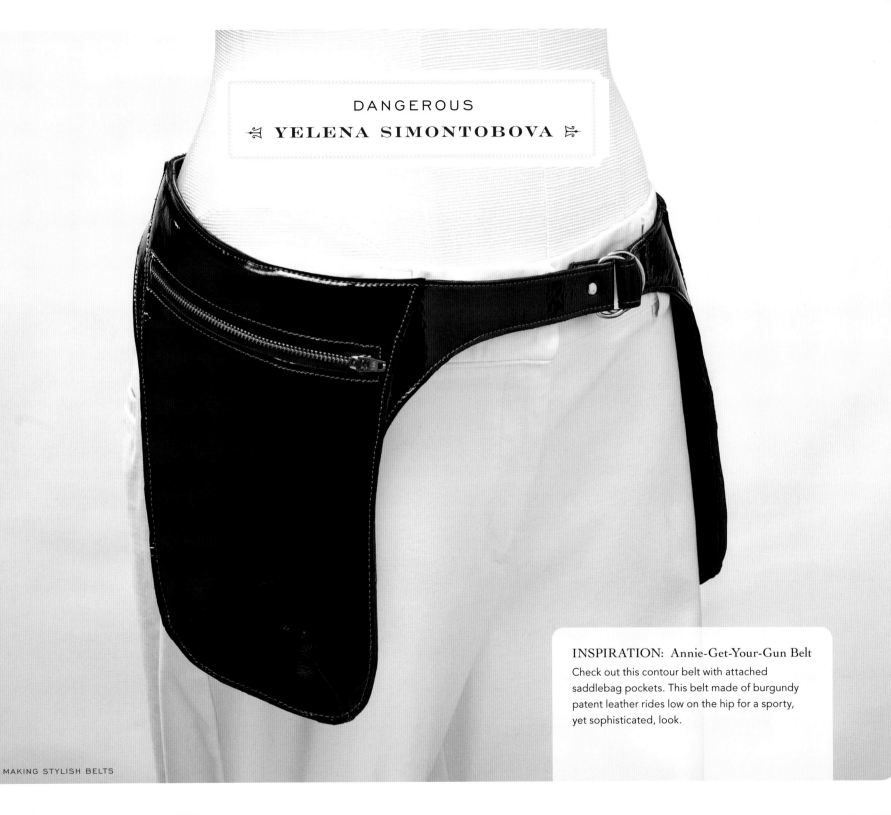

DANGEROUS

✥ YELENA SIMONTOBOVA ✥

INSPIRATION: Annie-Get-Your-Gun Belt

Check out this contour belt with attached
saddlebag pockets. This belt made of burgundy
patent leather rides low on the hip for a sporty,
yet sophisticated, look.

LE FLEUR AND FIFI LE FLEUR
❧ TOMOKO SEKIGUCHI ❧

INSPIRATION: Modified Raw-Edge and Turned-Edge Belts

In this day and age when consumers coordinate their accessories with those of their pets, why not do yours in style? This collection of purchased raw-edged belts is accentuated with silk-screened floral leather and studs on the pet collar. Just the right class and pizzazz!

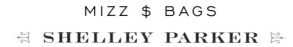

MIZZ $ BAGS
❧ SHELLEY PARKER ❧

INSPIRATION: Modified Raw-Edge Belt

In the case of this detachable money-pouch belt, simplicity, combined with a sassy silver appliqué, says it all. The pocket pouch is attached with a snap for easy removal. Make the pocket in a contrasting color for additional impact.

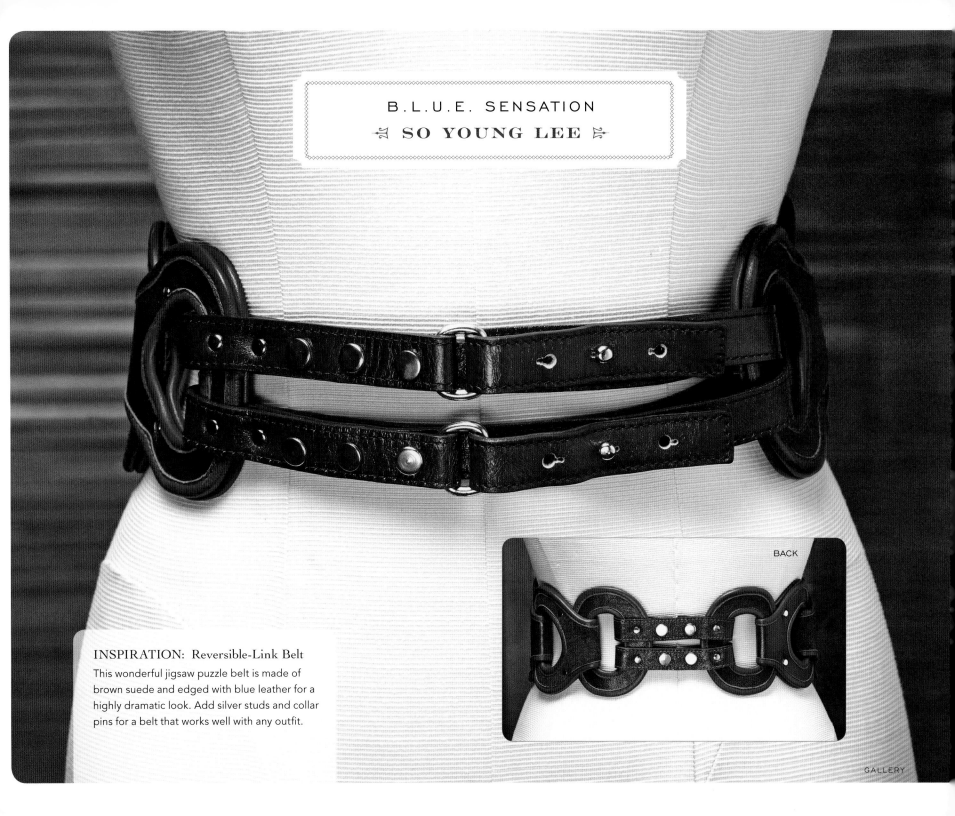

B.L.U.E. SENSATION
⌖ SO YOUNG LEE ⌖

BACK

INSPIRATION: Reversible-Link Belt

This wonderful jigsaw puzzle belt is made of brown suede and edged with blue leather for a highly dramatic look. Add silver studs and collar pins for a belt that works well with any outfit.

GALLERY

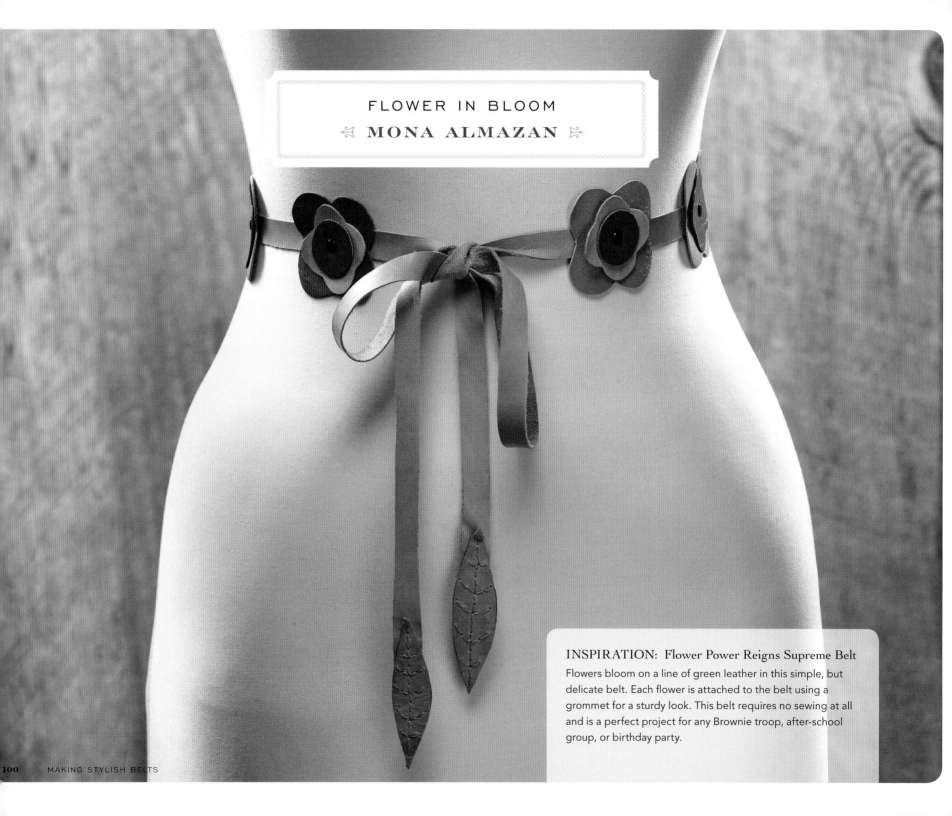

FLOWER IN BLOOM
❧ MONA ALMAZAN ❧

INSPIRATION: Flower Power Reigns Supreme Belt
Flowers bloom on a line of green leather in this simple, but delicate belt. Each flower is attached to the belt using a grommet for a sturdy look. This belt requires no sewing at all and is a perfect project for any Brownie troop, after-school group, or birthday party.

TSUBAKI AND ARWEN
TOMOKO SEKIGUCHI

INSPIRATION: Flower Power Reigns Supreme Belt

The title of the top belt, "Tsubaki," means "camellia" and that is exactly what this black-and-white flower belt represents. The black-and-white version is made of different fabrics sewn together and accentuated with a pearl center, and is attached to satin cording. The blue and white floral belt, "Arwen," is made of cut leather piled high with a tassel center and is laced with plastic tubing. Both belts offer completely different interpretations on the traditional flower-power belt.

TURNED BLUE
❧ SHELLEY PARKER ❧

INSPIRATION: Tablecloth-Sash Belt

What woman doesn't own at least one pair of blue denim jeans? And, more important, wouldn't you just love to change that rugged look of the jeans by adding one special belt? Here's the solution—this reversible denim sash is absolutely the perfect accessory.

LIZZY
❧ JEWEL LEE ❧

INSPIRATION: Waist Cincher Belt

Lizzy is a cinch belt with a lizard twist. Adding embossed lizard patches to a premade piece of cinched material and a belted closure makes this belt striking and completely original.

NEON AND ELECTRIC
⚓ SHELLEY PARKER ⚓

INSPIRATION: Raw-Edge Belt

Here are two similar raw-edge belts with totally different looks. "Neon" is made of lime green leather with a white painted edge for a show-stopping look, while "Electric" is a blue leather belt with coordinated edge paint but sporting electrifying zigzag accent stitching along the edges. Either one you choose is sure to be a major statement.

FLOWER TO THE PEOPLE
❧ ALLISON DENT ❧

INSPIRATION: Flower Power Reigns Supreme Belt

What an amazing double-wrapped belt! Made from store-bought trim and laced with leather, this belt takes on an exotic look. Add to that some hand-cut flowers, and you've got a floral statement that is extraordinary.

EASTERN COWGIRL
❧ SHELLEY PARKER ❧

INSPIRATION: Pleated Obi Belt

What fun to take a bit of the Orient and translate it to the American West! Shelley's obi has the look and feel of tradition with its pleated front, but the fabric sports an American cowgirl and has a huge tassel accent. Top that off with the fact that this belt is reversible and the tassel can be detached, and you have one amazingly functional and fabulous creation!

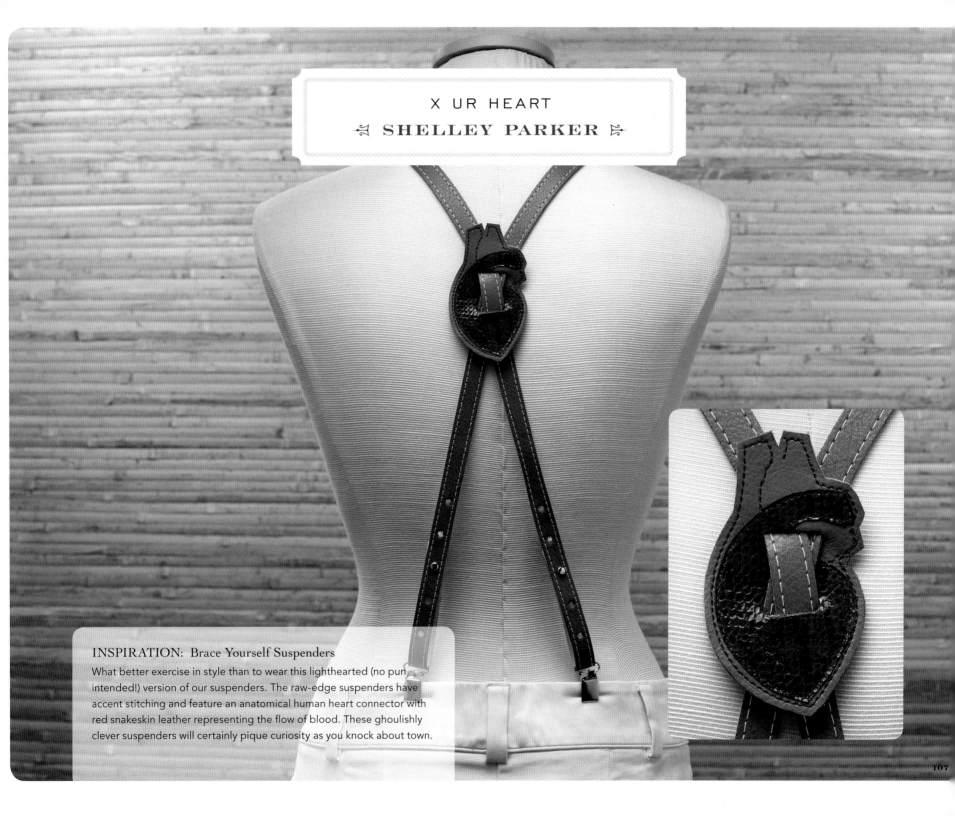

X UR HEART
SHELLEY PARKER

INSPIRATION: Brace Yourself Suspenders

What better exercise in style than to wear this lighthearted (no pun intended!) version of our suspenders. The raw-edge suspenders have accent stitching and feature an anatomical human heart connector with red snakeskin leather representing the flow of blood. These ghoulishly clever suspenders will certainly pique curiosity as you knock about town.

TIDAL WAVE
⚞ SHELLEY PARKER ⚟

INSPIRATION: Reversible-Link Belt
Made of three-toned suede, this linked belt
is sure to send ripples of style through any
wardrobe. Notice the contrasting belt buckle
for added impact.

PATTERNS

RAW-EDGE-BELT TEST STRIPS

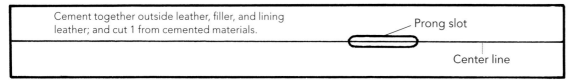

Cement together outside leather, filler, and lining leather; and cut 1 from cemented materials.

Prong slot

Center line

RAW-EDGE-BELT TEST STRIP FOR 3/4" (2 CM)-WIDE BUCKLE

Cement together outside leather, filler, and lining leather; cut 1 from cemented materials.

Prong slot

Center line

RAW-EDGE-BELT TEST STRIP FOR 1" (2.5 CM)-WIDE BUCKLE

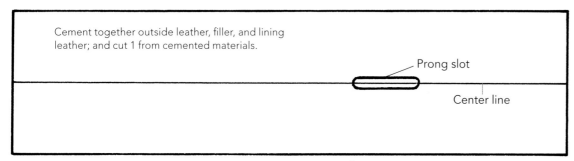

Cement together outside leather, filler, and lining leather; and cut 1 from cemented materials.

Prong slot

Center line

RAW-EDGE-BELT TEST STRIP FOR 1 1/2" (4 CM)-WIDE BUCKLE

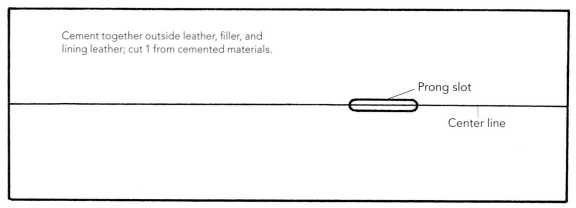

Cement together outside leather, filler, and lining leather; cut 1 from cemented materials.

Prong slot

Center line

RAW-EDGE-BELT TEST STRIP FOR 2" (5 CM)-WIDE BUCKLE

TURNED-EDGE-BELT TEST STRIPS FOR VARIOUS-WIDTH BUCKLES

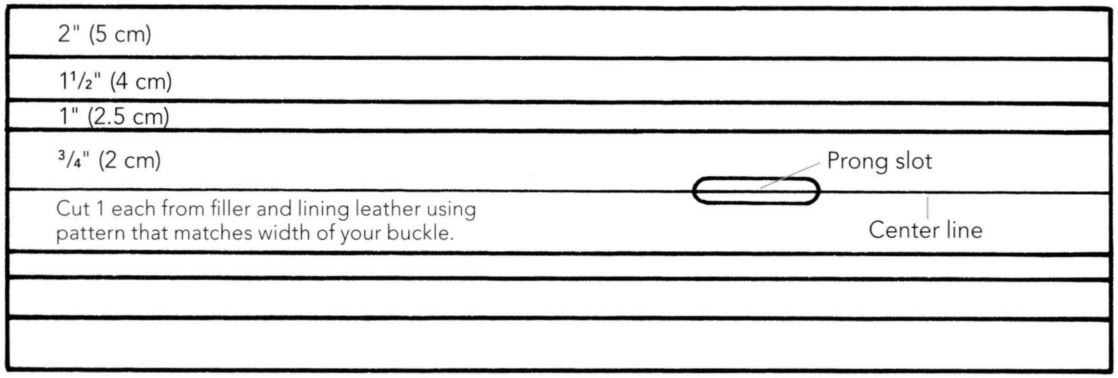

2" (5 cm)

1¹⁄₂" (4 cm)

1" (2.5 cm)

³⁄₄" (2 cm)

Prong slot

Cut 1 each from filler and lining leather using
pattern that matches width of your buckle.

Center line

FILLER AND LINING PATTERN

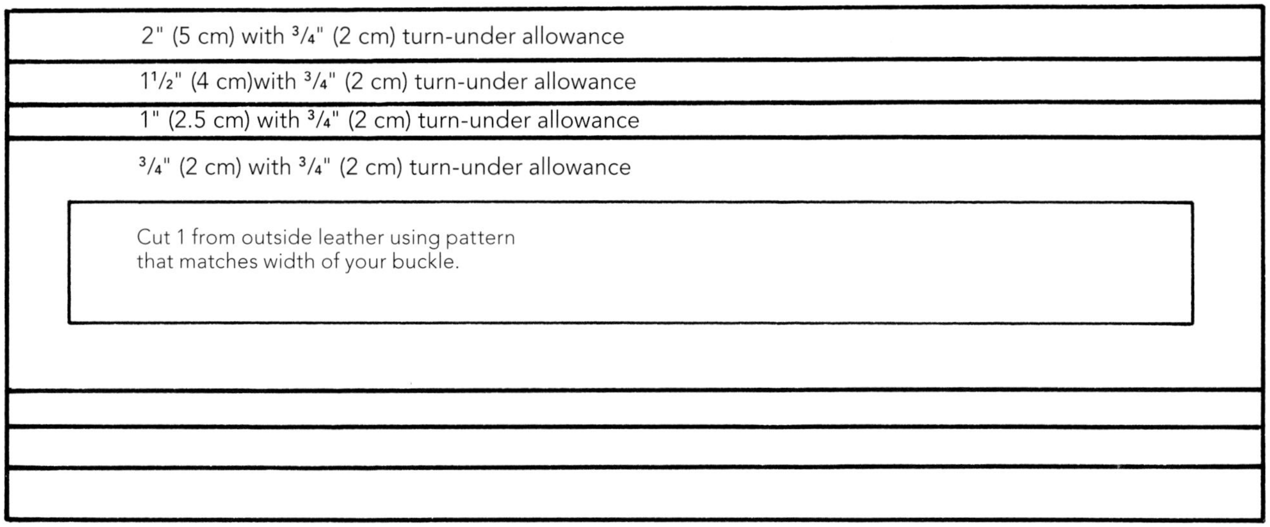

2" (5 cm) with ³⁄₄" (2 cm) turn-under allowance

1¹⁄₂" (4 cm) with ³⁄₄" (2 cm) turn-under allowance

1" (2.5 cm) with ³⁄₄" (2 cm) turn-under allowance

³⁄₄" (2 cm) with ³⁄₄" (2 cm) turn-under allowance

Cut 1 from outside leather using pattern
that matches width of your buckle.

OUTSIDE LEATHER PATTERN

TABLECLOTH-SASH BELT

Slit

Slit

Slit

Slit

Cut 1 in Leather.

Slit

Slit

Slit

Slit

OUTSIDE BUCKLE

Cut 1 from cardboard and 1 from leather.

Trapunto petal placement

OUTSIDE BUCKLE

Cut 4 trapunto petals from craft foam.

INSIDE BUCKLE PETAL

SLIT-PLAITED BELT

Rivet hole

Extend pattern for a total of seventeen 1" (2.5 cm) ovals spaced 1" (2.5 cm) apart

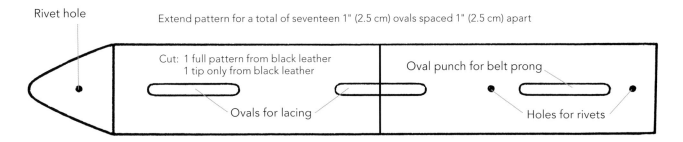

Cut: 1 full pattern from black leather
1 tip only from black leather

Oval punch for belt prong

Ovals for lacing

Holes for rivets

PATTERN FOR BLACK LEATHER

Extend pattern for a total of seventeen 1" (2.5 cm) ovals spaced 1" (2.5 cm) apart

Rivet hole

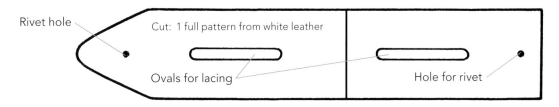

Cut: 1 full pattern from white leather

Ovals for lacing

Hole for rivet

PATTERN FOR WHITE LEATHER

PICTURE THIS! BELT

To complete pattern, continue window repeat for a total of 17 windows, including Section B.

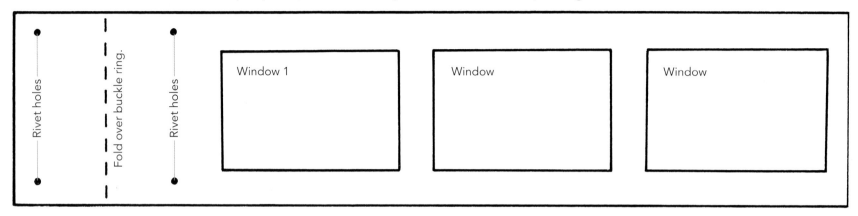

PHOTO BELT — SECTION A

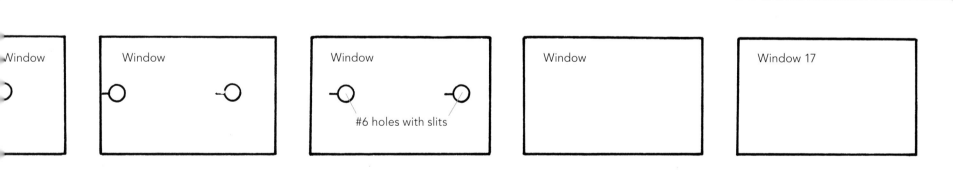

PHOTO BELT — SECTION B

PICTURE THIS! BELT

BELT BUCKLE LINING

Lining: Cut 1 along dotted line from thin black leather.

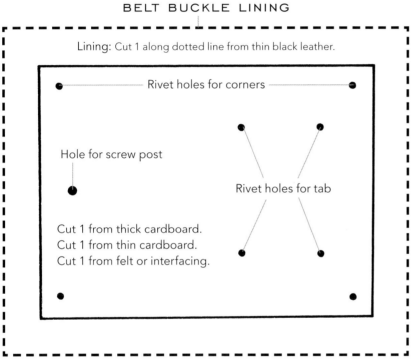

Rivet holes for corners

Hole for screw post

Rivet holes for tab

Cut 1 from thick cardboard.
Cut 1 from thin cardboard.
Cut 1 from felt or interfacing.

BELT BUCKLE MASTER PATTERN

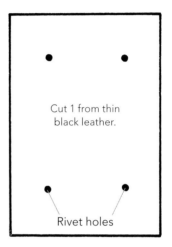

Cut 1 from thin black leather.

Rivet holes

TAB FOR RING

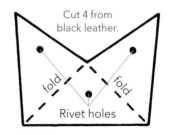

Cut 4 from black leather.

fold   fold

Rivet holes

BELT BUCKLE CORNER

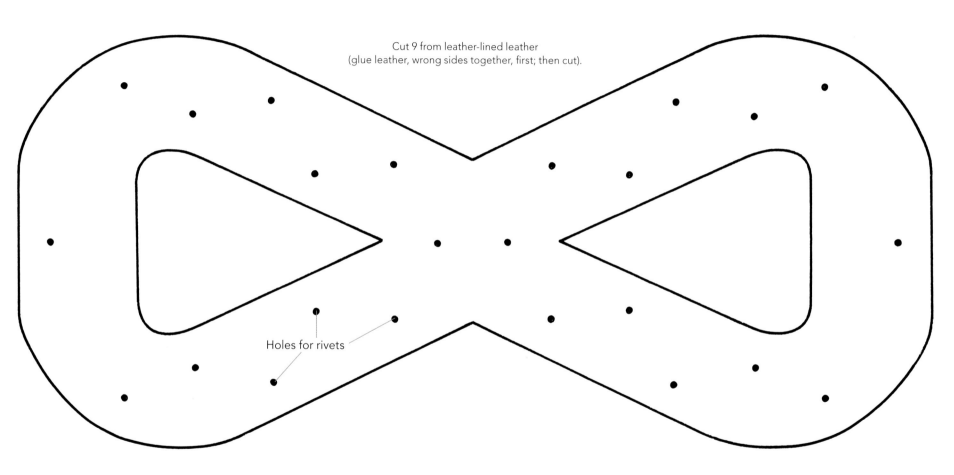

Cut 9 from leather-lined leather
(glue leather, wrong sides together, first; then cut).

Holes for rivets

LINK

REVERSIBLE-LINK BELT

Photocopy at 200%

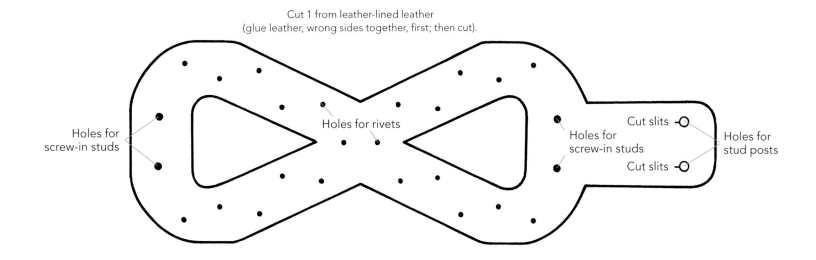

Cut 1 from leather-lined leather
(glue leather, wrong sides together, first; then cut).

Holes for
screw-in studs

Holes for rivets

Holes for
screw-in studs

Cut slits

Cut slits

Holes for
stud posts

LINK WITH CLOSURE

PLEATED OBI BELT

Photocopy at 200%

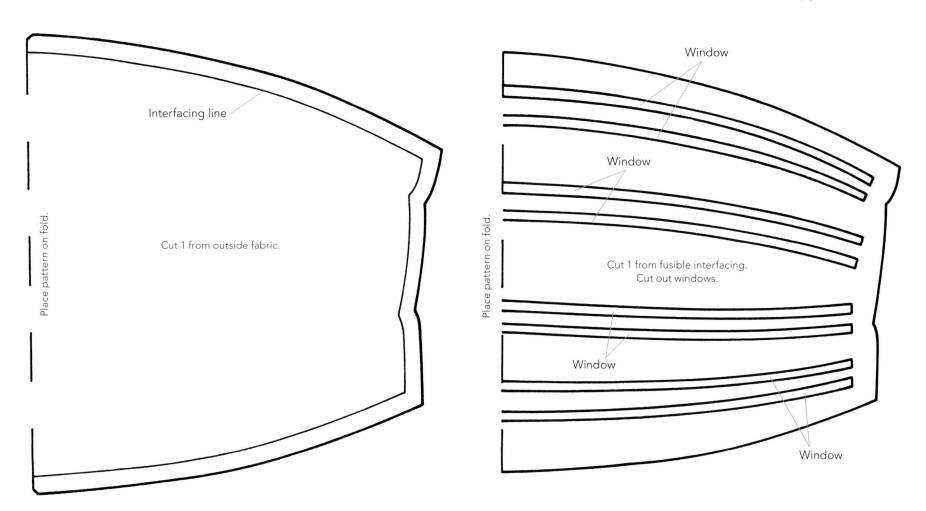

Interfacing line

Place pattern on fold.

Cut 1 from outside fabric.

Window

Window

Window

Window

Place pattern on fold.

Cut 1 from fusible interfacing.
Cut out windows.

PATTERN FOR FRONT OF BELT

FUSIBLE-INTERFACING
PATTERN FOR FRONT OF BELT

PLEATED OBI BELT

Photocopy at 200%

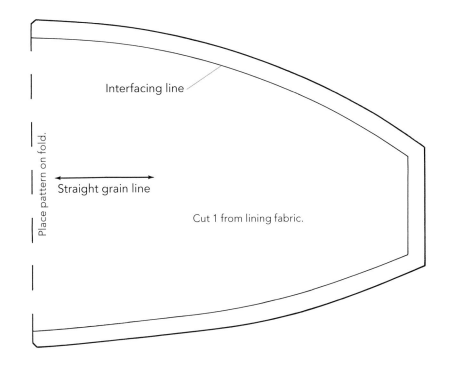

Interfacing line

Place pattern on fold.

Straight grain line

Cut 1 from lining fabric.

LINING PATTERN

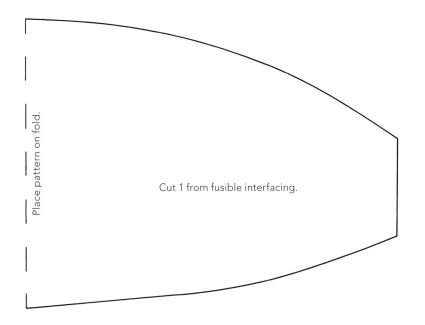

Place pattern on fold.

Cut 1 from fusible interfacing.

FUSIBLE-INTERFACING
PATTERN FOR LINING

TARTAN TIME BELT

Photocopy at 200%

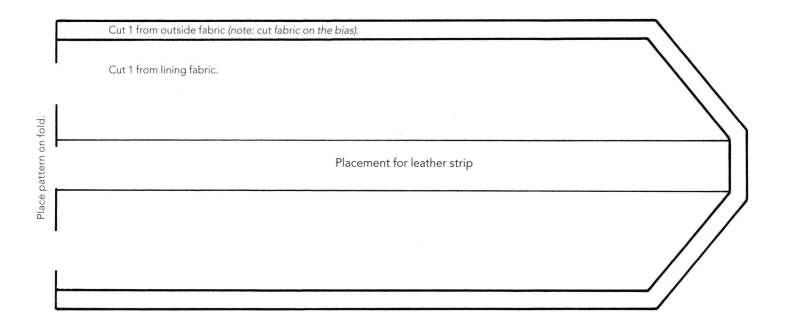

Cut 1 from outside fabric (*note: cut fabric on the bias*).

Cut 1 from lining fabric.

Place pattern on fold.

Placement for leather strip

FABRIC BELT AND LINING

TARTAN TIME BELT

Photocopy at 200%

Section A	Section B
Fold-under allowance.	
Cut 1 from leather.	—— Add 24" (61 cm) between sections A and B.
Fold-under allowance.	

LEATHER STRIP

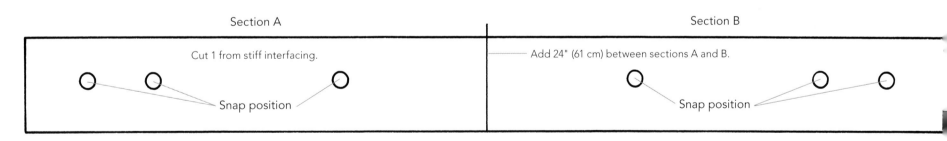

INTERFACING STRIP

FLOWER POWER REIGNS SUPREME BELT

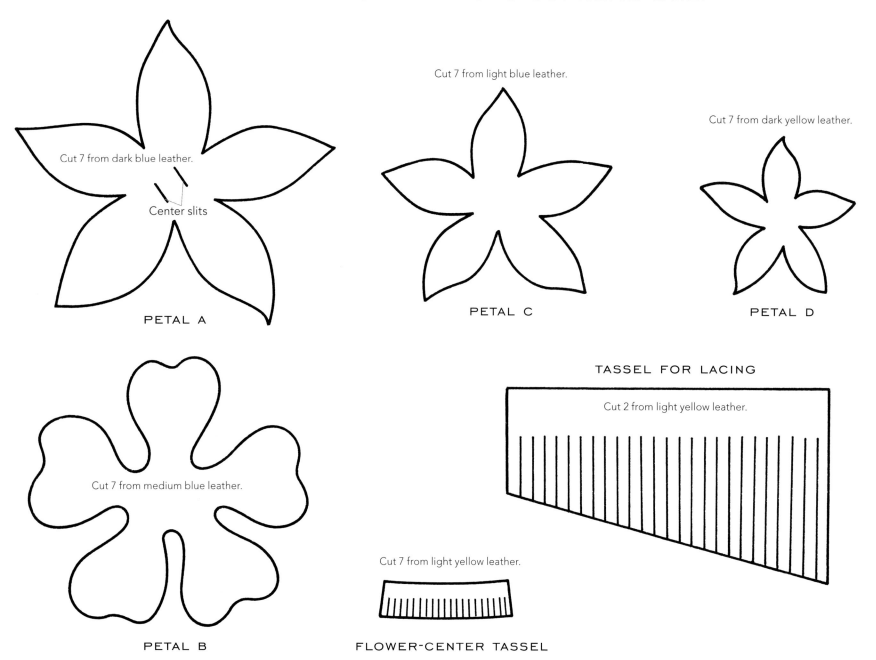

Cut 7 from dark blue leather.

Center slits

PETAL A

Cut 7 from light blue leather.

PETAL C

Cut 7 from dark yellow leather.

PETAL D

Cut 7 from medium blue leather.

PETAL B

TASSEL FOR LACING

Cut 2 from light yellow leather.

Cut 7 from light yellow leather.

FLOWER-CENTER TASSEL

X MARKS THE SPOT

BRACE YOURSELF SUSPENDERS

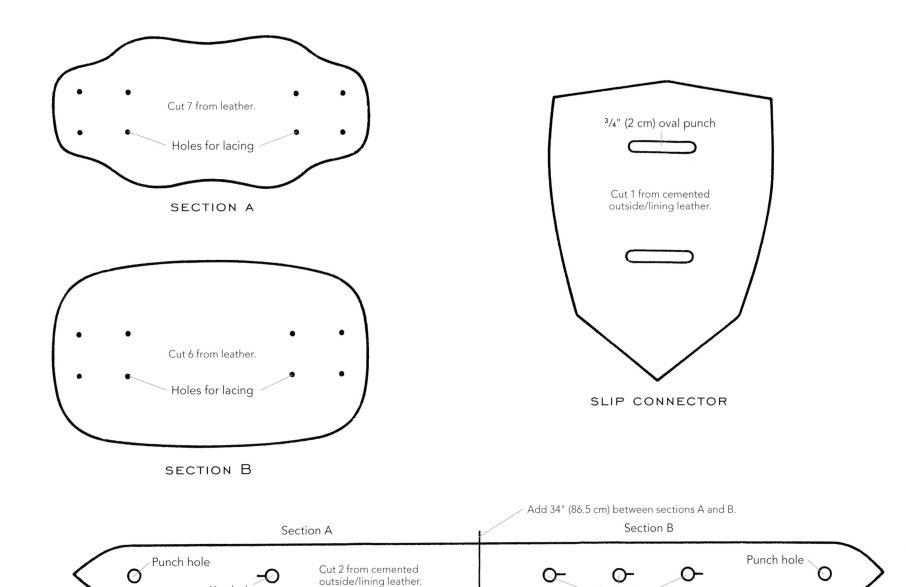

Cut 7 from leather.

Holes for lacing

SECTION A

Cut 6 from leather.

Holes for lacing

SECTION B

³/₄" (2 cm) oval punch

Cut 1 from cemented outside/lining leather.

SLIP CONNECTOR

Add 34" (86.5 cm) between sections A and B.

Section A

Section B

Punch hole

Key hole

Cut 2 from cemented outside/lining leather.

Key holes

Punch hole

SUSPENDER STRAPS

ANNIE-GET-YOUR-GUN CONTOUR BELT

Photocopy at 200%

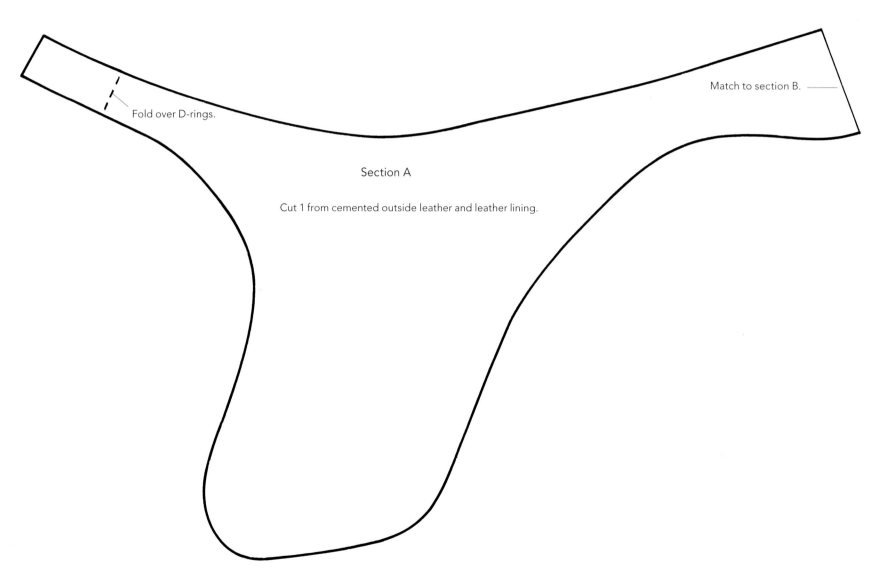

Fold over D-rings.

Match to section B.

Section A

Cut 1 from cemented outside leather and leather lining.

CONTOUR BELT AND INNER-POCKET BAG

ANNIE-GET-YOUR-GUN CONTOUR BELT

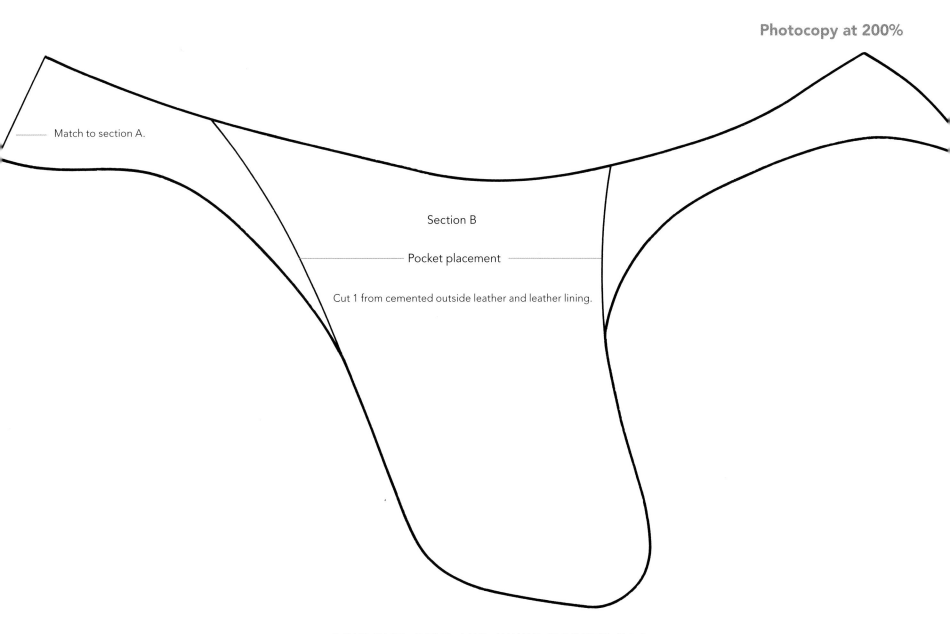

Photocopy at 200%

Match to section A.

Section B

Pocket placement

Cut 1 from cemented outside leather and leather lining.

CONTOUR BELT AND INNER-POCKET BAG

ANNIE-GET-YOUR-GUN CONTOUR BELT

Photocopy at 200%

Cut out window for zipper.

Cut 2 from cemented outside
leather and leather lining.

Be sure to flip pattern to cut
second pocket bag.

Tuck under

Tuck under

Slit

Slit

OUTER POCKET BAG

RESOURCES

BUCKLES

2Bhip
www.2bhipbuckles.com

Amazing Belt Buckles
www.amazingbeltbuckles.com

BeltBuckles
www.beltbuckles.ca

Belts Direct
www.beltsdirect.com

Buckle Shop
www.buckleshop.com

Buckle Warehouse
www.bucklewarehouse.com

Funky Buckles
www.funkybuckles.com

One Stop Candle
www.onestopcandle.com

Standing Bear's Trading Post
www.sbearstradingpost.com

Wholesale-Belt.com
www.wholesale-belt.com

LEATHER AND BUCKLES

Jinjiang Guotai Leather Co., Ltd.
www.guotai-leather.com

JustLeather.com
www.justleather.com

Le Prevo Leathers
www.leprevo.co.uk

LeatherGoodsConnection.com
www.leathergoodsconnection.com

Newberger Bros., Inc.
www.newbros.com

Springfield Leather Co.
www.springfieldleather.com

Tannerie Rémy Carriat
www.carriat.com

WBC Industries
www.wbcindustries.com

GENERAL

Ansun Multitech India Ltd.
www.ansun.com
belt hardware

Anteo
www.anteosrl.com
hardware catalog

Best-Price.com
www.best-price.com
resource for vintage hardware

Cosmos s.n.c.
www.cosmosmetals.com
variety of hardware

Fancy Fittings Ltd.
www.fancyfittings.com
hardware

The Fashiondex, Inc.
www.fashiondex.com
*variety of resources for fabrics
and trims*

G. Goldberg Co.
www.shoeeyelets.com
wide variety of eyelet sizes and shapes

Hoggan's Custom Canvas & Leather
www.hoggans.com
canvas and leather

KM Metal
www.kwongmingmetal.com
catalog of hardware

www.leatherrunltd.com
leather and hardware supplier

OBI
www.obi.it
authentic Italian hardware

Purple Chain Ind Co., Ltd.
www.buckles.com.tw
buckles and hardware

Terry Stack Ltd.
www.terrystack.com
belt buckles and hardware

**UMX—Universal Mercantile
Exchange, Inc.**
www.umei.com
hardware supplies

Zack White Leather Company
www.eleatherworks.com
leather and hardware

CONTRIBUTORS

Mona Almazan
monalmazan@hotmail.com

Allison Dent
imjanest@earthlink.net

Heather Golden
goldenheather@gmail.com

Sonja Hodzode
senjahodzode@hotmail.com

Jewel Lee
jewelclee@yahoo.com

So Young Lee
ppiyah81@hotmail.com

Shelley Parker
inmyshoes@shelleyparker10002.com

Tomoko Sekiguchi
tomo_sekiguchi@hotmail.com

Yelena Simontobova
letbe457@yahoo.com

Diana Sullivan
d-sullivan724@hotmail.com

ABOUT THE AUTHORS

ELLEN GOLDSTEIN-LYNCH

Ellen Goldstein-Lynch is the chairperson of the accessories design department at the Fashion Institute of Technology in New York City. She has been involved in the accessories field for more than twenty-five years and has served as public relations director for the National Fashion Accessories Association for ten years. She is an authority on handbags and accessories and has been featured on national television and in print.

NICOLE MALONE

Nicole Malone is an accessories designer with a passion for handbags. Her past freelance experience includes pattern making; sample making; and making custom, one-of-a-kind creations for various handbag and fashion designers. A graduate of the Accessories Design Program at the Fashion Institute of Technology, she currently designs and produces her own line of handbags and belts, but her true love is teaching in the accessories department at her alma mater.

SARAH MULLINS

Sarah Mullins is a graduate and faculty member of the accessories design department at the Fashion Institute of Technology. Sarah does freelance design for several New York City–based companies and also has her own line of unique handbags. Her passion is experimenting with different combinations of materials in her designs.

ACKNOWLEDGMENTS

Creativity is the ability to turn something mundane into something marvelous! Thanks to my co-authors for making that possible, to the wonderful people at Quarry Books for continuing to pitch great ideas to us, to my colleagues and students at FIT for getting the creative juices flowing, and also to my friends and family—thank you for allowing me to follow my dreams. It has been an amazing ride so far!

—Ellen Goldstein-Lynch

My family is so important to me, and I know how truly blessed I am for having them—to my amazing parents who always support me and make me feel like I am the best thing in the whole wide world. I love you so much! To my very cool brother and sister, Peter and Patti, my gorgeous and talented nieces, Shannon and Erin, and my wonderful father-in-law, Dad Malone.
Ellen, I cannot stress enough how grateful I am for your constant support, with this book and in many other areas of my life. Sarah, I am always amazed at your abilities to juggle around millions of things and make them all work out perfectly, and still find time to be such a good friend. Shelley, you make work fun and after work "funner." (Your stuff is so good that you're really starting to make me look bad—knock it off!) Carole, you are such a close soul to me in this life (just like you were in the former one). And thank you to all of my colleagues and former instructors.
To my students and all of you accessory designers out there, your dedication and creativity always motivates me to do what I do and to love every minute of it!
To Mary Ann, Rochelle, Christine, and all of the great people at Quarry Books; none of this could have been done without you.
To Brian Reiser…you are the most beautiful, caring, supportive friend in the whole wide world; I love you. And last, but not least, to my wonderful husband, Kevin, my love and best friend in the whole world; I love you always.
Oh yeah, I almost forgot Shooky!

—Nicole Malone

Thank you Ellen and Nicole for another creative endeavor. I hope we have many more collaborations in our future. To Mary Ann, Christine and everyone at Quarry Books, thank you for the opportunity to work together on one more fun project.
There are three names credited for this book, yet so many more people have given me their support. My list fits into two categories: Family (you'll find them in New York, Pittsburgh, Boston, Washington DC, Seattle and Point Roberts), and Friends (who can be found at FIT, Headgear, Oslo, Dory, The Metropolitan Museum, and the New York Post). I love you all, especially Alex and Ollie.

—Sarah Mullins